LIBRARIAN
TALES

Published in Partnership with ALA Editions

LIBRARIAN TALES

FUNNY, STRANGE, AND INSPIRING DISPATCHES FROM THE STACKS

WILLIAM OTTENS

Skyhorse Publishing

Skyhorse Publishing books may be purchased in bulk at special discounts for sales promotion, corporate gifts, fund-raising, or educational purposes. Special editions can also be created to specifications. For details, contact the Special Sales Department, Skyhorse Publishing, 307 West 36th Street, 11th Floor, New York, NY 10018 or info@skyhorsepublishing.com.

Skyhorse® and Skyhorse Publishing® are registered trademarks of Skyhorse Publishing, Inc.®, a Delaware corporation.

Visit our website at www.skyhorsepublishing.com.

10 9 8 7 6 5 4 3 2 1

Library of Congress Cataloging-in-Publication Data is available on file.

Cover design by Mona Lin
Cover photo credit Getty Images

ISBN: 978-1-5107-5588-8
Ebook ISBN: 978-1-5107-5589-5

Printed in the United States of America

To my mother, Linda, who always said I'd write a book someday. Thank you for believing in me.

Contents

Introduction

Where Are the Books?

Picture it: A reference desk situated in the center of the library, surrounded by stacks of books. I'm doing my normal librarian thing when a patron shuffles up and braces herself by placing both hands on the desktop. She takes a breath.

"Where are the books?" she says.

I blink.

She continues: "You know, the ones on DVD? That you can play in your car?"

She tilts her head as I furrow my brow and process her question in my overly technical head. *Books on DVD? That you play in your car?*

Then it hits me. *Oh! Audiobooks. On CD.*

I try not to laugh as I lead her to what she wants.

As a recently hired reference assistant at the Lawrence Public Library, I quickly learned that interactions at the desk, what librarians typically call reference interviews, are like putting together puzzles. Sometimes, not all the pieces are there. Other times, you completely misinterpret the situation.

At another library, at another reference desk, a young boy approaches and announces, "I'm looking for adventures!"

How adorable! I think to myself.

"Do you have adventures?" The kid continues.

"Of course! We have many adventures!" I respond. "What kind of adventures are you looking for?"

"No," the kid says, "AVENGERS. Do you have the Avengers?"

I smack my forehead.

Simple, silly moments like these convinced me that there would never be a dull day working at the library.

Contrary to popular belief, a librarian's job isn't always the quiet, easy, and stress-free paradise some movies, TV shows, and commercials portray it to be. We have our moments too, and that's partly because we work with the public, and anyone who works with the public should know things can get weird.

Unhappy patron contesting a 15-cent fine? Picture book with its corners gnawed off? Unattended toddlers ransacking the shelves? Dead bird in the book drop? All in a day's work.

After sharing a few of these stories on Facebook and getting some laughs from my family and friends, I decided to start a Tumblr called *Librarian Problems*.

It was 2012. GIFs were seeing a resurgence on the Internet, especially through reaction blogs on Tumblr. Inspired by others I'd come across, I started pairing common librarian situations, frustrations, and stereotypes with these animated images from popular TV shows, movies, and Internet videos. And it took off.

With consistent posting, the blog gained more than 2,000 followers in less than a month. Then I started receiving comments like this:

> *I think you're great! I mean really, really great! Did I say, "I think you're great"? No really, I'm not just flattering you, I really think you're great! Seriously though, thank you for providing a venue for me to laugh at my "problems". By the way, I think you're great!*

And like this:

I love your blog. I love your job. I love your sense of humor. SO obviously, I'm following you now :D This is so fun! You are so lucky to be a librarian. One of my dream jobs when I was a kid. I need to go to a library!!! ;p

And this one!

I'm just a library clerk, not a librarian. But I SO relate to pretty much everything here. I have been screamed at over a 25-cent fine. I've had creepy patrons invite me back to their house. Anyway, I love this blog and I want to give you all a big hug cause believe me, I understand!

That was it. I knew I had to keep at it. The likes, reblogs, comments, and followers kept coming, and I eventually expanded the *Librarian Problems* platform to Facebook and Twitter. I started handing out t-shirts and swag at conferences and received invitations to give keynote speeches. I loved talking about my problems.

Fast scroll through a few years and several pages of posts, and now you're reading this book! And what's this book about?

ALL MY PROBLEMS!

Just kidding. Sort of.

Since I haven't figured out how to print a GIF, these dispatches from the stacks, my librarian tales, will walk you through my library journey. I share how I first became interested in librarianship and then take you from library school, where all my problems began, to my brief stint as a director of a small library, where my problems grew exponentially.

You'll learn the good, the bad, and the ugly of working in five common library departments: circulation, reference, youth services, tech support, and collection services. And because I'm just one librarian, and I in no way represent the whole of librarianship, I've also thrown in some of the weird and wonderful stories shared through comments on the *Librarian Problems* pages.

Librarians and library workers manage a wide range of responsibilities, collections, and services, but we have one thing in common: we all see our fair share of problems.

Seriously, though, librarianship is no joke. We librarians and library workers are the gatekeepers to information. We keep the world in order. We provide vital resources and services to the most disadvantaged in our society. And the not so disadvantaged.

We see some gross stuff. Literally.

We also see how important our role and the role of our institutions are in our communities, and, for the most part, couldn't imagine ourselves doing any other thing. That's why, when you love your job so much, it helps to turn to laughter when things get tough. To let off steam. To share your problems. So you can go back and do your thing.

And that's what this book is all about.

So please, enjoy my librarian tales. They can be yours too.

Part I:

Where All My Problems Began

Chapter 1

Every Bookish Kid's Dream
(or One Librarian's Path)

"*Why are you interested in a master's degree in library science, William?*"

Sitting in a cozy chair across from the program director of the School of Library and Information Management at Emporia State University, I pause at this question. I should know this. I practiced this.

I pluck a strand of cat hair off my wool cardigan and then stare at the pencil holder on her desk. I was so nervous about the application interview, I convinced myself I needed to dress the part. Not smart. And yeah, I admit my knowledge of

librarianship relied on stereotypes perpetuated by pop culture.
I feel the sweat dripping down my sides.

"I've never been more comfortable than in a room with
books," I say.

Really? William. Come on.

"I love teaching and sharing knowledge..."

Here I go, rambling again.

"...and I've always loved books."

Did I just lie?

If the program director suspected, she didn't show it. She
smiled and nodded, and the interview continued. Spoiler alert:
I got into library school. But that's not exactly where all my
problems began.

As a hiring manager now, I often get cover letters
that begin something like, "To whom it may concern:
I have loved books and reading since I was a small
child. My earliest and fondest memories are of trips
to the library..."

That's not my story. My parents didn't read to
me regularly, and the only memories I have of my
small-town library are of the frowning library aides
who watched my every move and told me not to sit
in certain areas. I came to fear checking out books
because our visits were few and far between, and I
didn't want to be admonished for late fees.

The public library was a small brick building two blocks away from the elementary school. A circulation desk faced the center aisle between two rows of stacks, and study tables and chairs were situated in the aisle. A reading area was positioned behind the stacks. The few memories I do have consist of sitting shyly in the back at storytime activities in the program room and checking out scratch and sniff picture books (the hygienics of which I only now realize were questionable at best).

One encounter when I was in middle school, though, turned me off. I had walked to the library after school to do a bit of studying and found a quiet space at a table in the back. After cracking open my math book, I looked up to find one of the library aides approaching my table. She crossed her arms, glared down at me, and asked, "What are you doing here?"

"I'm studying," I said. "Am I not supposed to be here?"

"This is the adult area."

I looked around. There weren't any adults in the area. Other than the library aide, I was alone.

"Why aren't you in the teen area?"

I stared at her. She pointed down the main aisle. "It's in front of the stacks."

I assumed she was referring to the single high-top table near the one shelf of young adult novels in clear sight of the circulation desk. Yeah, no thanks.

"So, I can't be here?"

"Well, I guess you'll be fine. Just be quiet."

With that, she walked away. I couldn't figure out why it mattered when there weren't any adults wanting to use my table, and I wasn't bothering anyone. I decided then that, if I couldn't sit, quietly that is, without being accosted by a library aide, the place wasn't for me.

Despite my disdain for the public library, though, a love of books and a desire to become a librarian developed in my teenage years. It was kind of a romantic fantasy.

It all started when I joined the book club sponsored by the high school librarian, Ms. Bahm. Each month, members got a free copy of a selected book, and the group would discuss the reading over dinner or watch a movie based on it.

Free books, free food, and free movies—who could resist?

I appreciated being surrounded by others who loved books and being able to geek out about them in a safe space. I admired Ms. Bahm for sponsoring the club and earning the grant money that paid for the books and food.

Oh, and I loved the books.

One novel, though, opened my eyes. After reading Billie Letts's *Where the Heart Is*, I secretly wanted to be Forney Hull, the surly, eccentric caretaker of the Sequoyah Public Library and love interest of the main character, Novalee Nation.

Letts's description of Forney led me to imagine myself reciting random facts and helping patrons, surrounded by ornate wood carved trim, chandeliers, and stacks and racks of books. At that point, though, it felt like a far-off dream. I first had to graduate high school and get through college, the latter of which was a rare accomplishment for my working-class family. Part of me feared I would never make good enough grades or have enough money to get there, and I'd end up working in a gas station or grocery store forever.

I did make it, though, and that dream shifted into becoming a teacher. My goal was to return to my hometown and "give back to the community" by getting a position in the school district. I chose Graceland University, a small private liberal arts school in southern Iowa, and intended to double major in elementary education and mathematics. When I shared this with my freshman guidance counselor, she laughed and told me I'd be there for ten years. I took that as a challenge.

Then, like with many undergrads, my plans changed.

As I began taking introductory education courses and getting involved in the student education association, I lost interest in the field. I learned about the *No Child Left Behind Act* and the increasing focus on standardized testing, and I no longer wanted to be a part of it. I still had a desire, though, to share knowledge and teach, but I didn't want to do so in a place where students were mandated by the government to be there. I wanted to work where people came because they wanted to learn.

Graceland's Frederick Madison Smith Library helped reignite that dream of becoming Forney Hull. The four floors of stacks, study carrels, and meeting spaces with floor to ceiling windows that overlooked the wooded hills on the edge of campus provided an oasis of silence and order away from the chaos of the dorms. Even on freezing winter nights, I would trudge along the walkways, lined with three feet of blown snowdrifts, between the dorms and the library to spend hours studying in the quiet stacks or reading in a cozy chair.

The impressive brick, concrete, and glass building was completed in the 1960s. In an interview I completed for a class project, the director of the library told me that the former library was on the third floor of another building on campus. When the new one was built, students and faculty formed a human chain, down the staircases and the hill between the two buildings, to pass the books, hand to hand, to the new library.

I wanted to be a part of a history like that.

When I learned that students could apply for work-study positions as reference assistants or circulation clerks, I was instantly jealous. I didn't qualify for the program, and while I could apply for remaining positions after all qualifying students had been placed, the few at the library were filled quickly. I begrudgingly found other positions on campus, but this inspired me to seriously investigate what it would take to get a library job when I finished my degree.

After college, I ended up working at a high school anyway. I got a position as a paraeducator, and I got a second job working overnight at a group home. Oh, and I worked weekends making pizza at a gas station. Ideally, I would have gone straight to grad school, but with thousands of dollars in student loans, I convinced myself I had to work three jobs to stay ahead. I didn't have the time or money for it.

It was rough. I would leave for the group home at 10:30 p.m., work for 8 hours, go straight to the high school at 7:30 a.m., work for another 8 hours, get home at 3:30 p.m. and get barely enough sleep before doing it all over again. Then I spent my weekends at the gas station.

It only took a year before I realized I could spend half my life exhausting myself, paying off the student loans and dreaming about becoming a librarian, or I could apply to graduate school and do it.

I remember being so intimidated by the School of Library and Information Management (SLIM)'s application process. First, I had to take the GRE. Then I had to get three reference letters. And then I had to sit through an interview with the program director. Each step of the way, my inner saboteur (to borrow a phrase from RuPaul) kept telling me it wasn't going to happen.

For the interview, I chose to wear a brown Lacoste wool cardigan that I bought at a second-hand vintage shop. Fake it 'til you make it, right? Thankfully, the program director was kind, patient with my rambling tendencies, and welcomed me into the School of Library and Information Science.

I was finally on my way to becoming ~~Forney Hull~~ a real librarian.

Chapter 2
Five Things I Learned in Library School

From what I can recall, SLIM's degree program was two years' worth of lengthy reading assignments, group projects, term papers, annotated bibliographies, and presentations. I don't mean to reduce it to that, but, hey, it's been about ten years!

It was billed as the perfect program for working adults. Generally, I had to take two courses per semester, and other than one weekend intensive per month, most of the classwork was done online. Now that I'm ten years out of it, though, it feels like it was a quick crash course in librarianship. Or a ten-minute YouTube video. I don't remember every detail of every course, but here are a few things that did stick with me:

Librarians come from all walks of life

I learned as early as orientation that not all librarians come from bookish backgrounds and have degrees in English literature. An ice breaker activity revealed interests in business administration, psychology, sociology, music, education, and law in my cohort alone.

Some of my classmates had been working in libraries as assistants, clerks, or paraprofessionals for years, while others had found their way to librarianship as a second or third (or even further) career.

For one of the sessions, the instructors brought in a panel of recently graduated librarians to share their experiences. One of the panelists said they had gone from public administration to tech jobs before going into libraries. Another said he had been working as a car salesman before he applied for a director position at the library in his small town.

The students in my cohort were also interested in working in different types of libraries. Emporia's program is suited for academic, school, special, and public librarians as well as archivists, and they all take the same core courses at the beginning. Later in the program, you start specializing in one specific area, or, like what I chose to do, you can take courses from different areas for more general education.

Because I still had some lingering interest in working in a school, I fell in with a group of students who wanted to become school librarians but didn't have a teaching degree to which to "attach" the masters. (In Kansas, we learned you had to have a teaching endorsement first, or work with youth for three years at a public library and then find a district willing to hire you on a restricted basis.) Even among this group, some wanted to work in middle or high schools and others who wanted to be elementary school librarians.

Who knew librarianship was so complex?

Everything I needed, I learned while working at a gas station

I made pizza and served ice cream at a gas station in my hometown as a part-time gig through high school and college. It was one of those jobs where you're expected to work constantly, even if there weren't any customers to help. The manager's motto was, "If you can see it, it needs to be cleaned."

Working at the gas station taught me how to work independently and with others, how to please customers and managers, and the importance of following directions. As I read course materials and participated in class discussions in library school, I couldn't help but draw connections between the gas station and librarianship.

From keeping the store organized so customers knew where to find things to the importance of providing positive customer service, there was a lot of overlap. We even watched Bob Farrell's "Give 'Em the Pickle!" customer service training video in Theoretical Foundations of Service. I swear I could have presented this, except it would have been "Give them the extra pepperoni!"

I learned a lot about human behavior at the gas station that translated well to the library too. At the gas station, when we ran out of chocolate ice cream, I would post a sign on the counter. Standing right next to that sign, customers would still ask for chocolate ice cream. Patrons do the same thing at the library! Internet down? Printer not working? Restrooms closed? Even with clear signage, you're going to have people asking.

Theory, coupled with practical experience, is best (for me, at least)

Theoretical Foundations of Service, Theory of Organization of Information, Organization Theories for Administering Information Agencies—ESU's graduate program was loaded with theory courses. While reading books and journal articles and discussing theories in class might give you an understanding of why libraries are operated the way they are, for me, practical experience alongside it was helpful.

When I started the program, I was still working as a paraeducator and had just begun applying for library positions. Many of the students in my cohort were already working in libraries, and I envied their ability to provide specific examples from their jobs in class discussions. I did the best I could to keep up, but when, in my second semester, I finally got my first library job, that's really when I felt like I was beginning to learn.

Directing patrons to the materials they were looking for helped me understand the theories about why humans organize things the way we do. S. R. Ranganathan's second law of library science, "Every person his or her book," was put into perspective when I was struggling through my first attempts at readers' advisory.

If I weren't directly seeing how some of those theories were being put into practice while I was learning them, they may not have stuck as well.

There are three types of people you'll work with on any group project

Whether it's an afternoon activity or a semester-long project, many library school courses will require you to work with a group. I've always been a fan of going it alone, but I've never quite figured out whether that's because I'm incredibly shy or because I am overconfident in my ability and prefer to do everything myself. Probably a combination.

My biggest group project was an exercise in developing a strategic plan for a fictional library in Organization Theories for Administering Information Agencies (basically "How to Manage a Library"). When the instructor assigns a group project worth fifty percent of the course grade, things get serious. Not only did I learn how to perform S.W.O.T. (Strengths, Weaknesses, Opportunities, and Threats) and P.E.S.T (Political, Economic, Socio-Cultural, and Technological) analyses, but I also discovered three types of people you'll work with on any group project.

First, there are the leaders. These students know exactly what must be done and are great at giving directions. They interpret assignment instructions, divide up the workload, and initiate discussions. If there's any confusion or questions about the project, they're the first to reach out to the instructor for assistance. They'll plan the project out through the final presentation and keep the group on task.

Then you have your achievers. The achievers will jump on the most significant portion of the work, and most likely complete it before anyone has a chance to even think about getting started on their own. Like the leaders, they're super organized and have plenty of initiative, but lack enough of it to let the real leaders run the show. Sometimes achievers and leaders are the same, and they often pick up the slack from the third group.

That third group is the procrastinators. Waiting until the last minute to do any work at all, these students usually contribute by doing the bare minimum. Sometimes, that contribution is giving an oral presentation. (No shade here! I understand, especially for introverts, the challenge of public speaking and how important this contribution is.) They may take some extra encouragement, a few emails, a desperate phone call, a prod from the professor, but eventually, they'll get some work done. Some people work best under pressure, right?

This is in no way an exhaustive list. Depending on the project, you may find yourself a leader, an achiever, a procrastinator, or somewhere in between. You may also find yourself frustrated or annoyed with the people you're working with. Whether you appreciate them or not, group projects are great for providing experience working with other people and, hopefully, teaching you more about yourself and your working style.

Library school doesn't end when your degree is in your hand

The most important thing I learned through the master's program was the fact that librarianship is a continually evolving field. As long as new technologies are developed, as long as people find new ways to consume information, and as long as new generations' values evolve, libraries and librarians will need to keep up with, if not be at the forefront of, that change. There will always be opportunities to learn something new, and thankfully, in what better place could we be than in organizations that are, inherently, about access to resources and lifelong education?

Chapter 3

I Need a Library Job: The Struggle Is Real

The library where I currently work is my first job. When a lady took medical leave they hired me temporarily. It was part-time, but I stuck with it, and finally this year I stepped into a full-time position and my dream job.

I know I am lucky, but I believe that sticking your neck out is worth it.

— Facebook comment

In my first year of grad school, when I was commuting to Lawrence, Kansas, and working at the high school, I would drive by the public library every day on my way home and tell myself, "Someday I'm going to work there."

Getting that job, though, was a bit tougher than I had imagined. With two high schools and a university, the job market in Lawrence was tough. It helped to have connections. I didn't.

I applied to several positions in different departments and never got a response. I also offered to volunteer, but even those opportunities were scarce and I was never called upon to help.

Figuring I'd have to start elsewhere, I applied for a circulation position at a small library in another town. I was thrilled when I got an interview and even more so when they called back for a second round. With my bachelor's degree and a solid start toward my masters, I figured the job was as good as mine.

How wrong I was.

The interview went...okay? It was my first ever in front of an entire committee. I swear even the janitor was there. I sat up straight, answered their questions as clearly and concisely as I could, and tried my best to exude confidence.

I got the call as soon as I stepped into my apartment, returning from the interview. I didn't even live fifteen minutes away.

"Hi William," the assistant director greeted me on the phone. "Thank you for your interest in this position. We thought you were great, but we've chosen to offer it to someone with more experience."

So that's what it feels like when the world lets you down.

This is when I almost gave up. I seriously started to believe that librarianship wasn't for me. That I was going to library school for nothing. But, clearly, I didn't give up that easily.

In my second semester of library school, I had to do an observation at a reference desk, and that's when things started to fall into place. I emailed the director of the Lawrence Public Library and asked if I could set up a time to observe at their desk. He referred me to Lynn, the adult services coordinator, who was happy to let me come in and watch for a bit.

Lynn happened to be covering the desk for a sick staff member when I arrived for my observation. She was very friendly and expressed interest in my schoolwork. We chatted for a while, I watched her interact with a couple of patrons, and I left with enough information to write my paper. When I visited the library's website for some follow-up information, I noticed there was an opening in Lynn's department. I promptly wrote her an email thanking her for allowing me to do the observation and mentioned that I would be applying.

Imagine my joy when I got the call for an interview!

Until those first few attempts at getting a position in a library, I had never felt a lack of confidence in interviewing and getting jobs. But now I had major self-esteem issues. Because I had already met Lynn, though, I was able to relax and feel comfortable speaking with her and the assistant director about my experience and the position.

Afterward, Lynn pretty much told me to expect a phone call. She had a few other interviews but said she had a good feeling about me. One thing that helped: there were a few other students from my class who completed observations in her department, but I was the only one who sent a thank-you note, and that impressed her. (Take note, job seekers!)

And so, a few days later, she called and offered me the part-time reference assistant position and my adventures, and my problems, at the Lawrence Public Library began!

Now fast forward three years, a promotion or two, and a few other life changes. I began to feel the itch to move on. Opportunities to advance further at LPL were scarce. I didn't foresee anyone retiring or leaving anytime soon, so I began to look for positions near my partner's family.

A director gig caught my eye. Not putting a lot of faith into it, I applied.

What board of trustees would hire a 27-year-old with only three years of reference experience behind him? I kept thinking as I waited for a response.

Apparently, the one that oversees the Oskaloosa Public Library would. It all started with a call from the city's HR clerk inviting me to interview with the board. Breaking the news to Lynn was difficult. Having developed a positive professional relationship, I had to be up front and honest about what was happening. When I told her I needed to take the weekend off for an interview on a Monday, she was dumbfounded.

"Why do you need a weekend to interview in Oskaloosa?" she asked.

I hadn't been clear. She thought I meant Oskaloosa, Kansas, which happens to be a thirty-minute drive away.

"It's actually Oskaloosa, Iowa," I admitted.

She looked away from me, tears forming in her eyes.

"I know you'll do great," she said. "You'll get this."

When the day came, I knew I botched the interview. After climbing the stairs of a beautifully renovated and expanded Carnegie building, I sat awkwardly outside a meeting room before being invited in to sit before the entire board and the city manager.

I checked my button-up shirt for sweat stains and entered.

Have you ever caught yourself rambling and then tried to find your way back to the point, but then forgot what the point was? Yeah, that was me with half the questions. But I did my best, and I put my little librarian heart on my sleeve.

After the interview, I walked down the stairs, greeted the staff member who let me in the building, and then saw an older gentleman in a nice three-piece suit who I assumed was the next interviewee.

Well, at least I tried, I said to myself.

Two weeks later, I got the call that brought my time at the Lawrence Public Library to an end. I was off to new and bigger problems as a library director!

Fast forward yet another three years, and my partner gets a job offer back in Lawrence at the University of Kansas Libraries. (Yes, librarianship is infectious.) Thus, I was on the hunt again. And this search proved to be eye-opening.

I started where I left. I applied and interviewed for a full-time position that happened to be available at the Lawrence Public Library.

They know me! I've got all this experience now. This should be easy.

Wrong.

Key tip: never get too comfortable.

At one point during the interview, I took a sip of water and someone said something funny that caused me to spit take. Water sprayed over the table and on the hiring supervisor. I like to blame my not getting the job on that incident.

And so, the search continued. I put in application after application. Children's librarian at a small library. Nothing. Information services assistant at a branch library in the Kansas City suburbs. Nothing. A director position at another small library. Close. I interviewed. Felt good. But again, they went with someone who had more experience.

Through all of that, I kept monitoring the jobs page on the Lawrence Public Library's website. Another full-time position opened, and through the process again I went. This time, after a phone interview, the hiring manager told me I failed to sell myself.

What's that even supposed to mean? I asked myself. *I'm a successful library director. My experience should speak for itself!*

I still had a lot to learn.

A part-time position in their reference department opened after that. I applied. I drove three hours to interview, again, with the same hiring manager. I thought I did better.

Nope. Not good enough to land that job.

At this point, I found myself doubting my abilities and doubting whether I should continue my career in librarianship. But then, the hiring manager reached out and encouraged me to apply for a part-time position in their new readers' services department.

Reluctantly, I did so. I promised myself this was the last attempt at LPL.

This time, I was prepared. This time, I sold myself. This time, a friend from library school was directly overseeing the new department, and thankfully, she had faith in my skills, experience, and potential. I finally got back to LPL as a part-time member of the Book Squad!

So that was my ~~struggle~~ library job hunting experience.

I know that I'm speaking from a place of privilege. Others spend much more time and emotional energy in their searches for library jobs. And I can't even speak to the unfair disadvantages that Black, Indigenous, and People of Color experience trying to get a position in this field.

My issue was hyper-localizing. If I wasn't so set on returning to the Lawrence Public Library, perhaps I could have found a position more quickly elsewhere. This is an issue that many unemployed librarians share. Not everyone can pick up and move across the country for a position.

To those still on the hunt, here's what I have to offer. These are the things I had to learn or remind myself through my job hunts:

Don't let one rejection (or five!) discourage you

There are a lot of fish in the sea, and there are a lot of librarians in the field. Jobless librarians. Experienced librarians. When there are hundreds of applicants for one position, there's a good chance that you may not measure up when compared to the others. But that doesn't mean you'll never measure up. The list of available library jobs may be small, but take the time and patience to apply, apply, apply!

Apply, apply, apply!

The more applications you put in, the more you can improve your resume, cover letter, and interview skills and the better the chance you'll have at getting a job. You may think there's a perfect job at the one perfect library, and you won't be happy anywhere else, but the time you spend waiting for that job to open at that one library is time you could be spending gaining experience elsewhere.

Learn how to sell yourself

You may think you have a reputation that precedes you. You may have great connections and references. However, just because you have volunteered or worked for a library before and have done a wonderful job doesn't mean you're a shoo-in. Each interview—even if it's with the same hiring supervisors repeatedly—is a new one. You've got a new crowd of applicants to compete against. Learn how to translate your skills and abilities to fit the position and be confident! You don't have to embellish, but explain how your years of serving tables or selling retail demonstrate your customer service skills, etc.

Be patient

Waiting to hear back on an application is the toughest part. I know. Some hiring processes are much slower than others—especially when there are a ton of applications to dig through. If you're concerned that they may not have received your application, it's okay to check in on it, but you don't have to call in every three days asking for an update. That's bugging. If you've sold yourself well enough in your application materials, they'll contact you.

Be grateful—and show it!

Hiring supervisors are busy, and the hiring process takes a lot of their time. If they give you an interview, close it by expressing your gratitude for their time and consideration. Sending a quick thank-you letter or email afterward is also nice too. It shows that you care enough about the position and that you're professional and considerate of their time. If you don't get the job, they may remember you for the next.

You may not get the job you want. I didn't at first, and it was tough. Then I got my dream job. Twice, in fact. Each time I entered the job market, I had my share of rejections, but I didn't let them discourage me completely.

To anyone who's looking, know there's a job out there for you—keep at it! You'll get there! Good luck!

Chapter 4

It's Like a Dream Come True: My First Library Job

"*Okay, now try doing an author search for Patricia Cornwell,*" *the reference assistant says.* "*Mouse over to the drop-down menu by the search bar and select author.*"

I grit my teeth and follow her instructions. I know this, I think. Just let me work on the reference desk. Please!

"*Nice! Now, limit the results to books by using the facets on the left.*"

Seriously? Do they not think I've used the catalog before?

I glance at my trainer to make sure she doesn't notice my irritation and continue following her directions. I have two whole weeks of orientation ahead of me, and I don't want to alienate her, as kind as she's been.

Whenever I reminisce about my first day at the Lawrence Public Library, I think of Disney's Cinderella in her ball gown, twirling and exclaiming, "Why it's like a dream! A wonderful dream come true." Swap out the ball gown and glass slippers with a cardigan and Chucks, and you've got my real-life fairy tale. Starry-eyed and ready to take on the reference desk, I didn't realize how fleeting that feeling would turn out to be.

Touring the workplace, meeting coworkers, filling out paperwork—no matter where you work, your first day can be a bit overwhelming. Getting started at the library was no exception.

Actual post from my Facebook memories:

July 15, 2009
William Ottens *is totally not overwhelmed with all that he's learned and is supposed to learn at the library!!! At least the coworkers are friendlyyy*

My orientation shift included meeting a few of my reference counterparts, going over my position description with my supervisor, reviewing the employee handbook with the bookkeeper, and filling out and signing more paperwork. From there, I was handed off to a member of the circulation staff who had volunteered to give tours to new hires.

Having only been in a few of the public spaces, I was excited to explore the whole building and venture into the staff areas. Completed in 1972 as a replacement for the original Carnegie building, the library featured exposed stone walls, a sunlit atrium, a children's room packed with overloaded shelves, a media room, and a lower level with overflow stacks, a computer lab, and staff offices. As we passed through the different departments, my tour guide introduced me to each staff member we encountered.

The Adult Services, Youth Services, and Circulation departments were on the main level. Technical Services, Acquisitions, and Collection Development workspaces were on the lower level, some in converted maintenance closets and hallways. The director's office, a staff lounge, and a facilities workshop were also downstairs, and the Friends of the Library group had a large space for storage and sorting for their annual book sale that overflowed into what was once a mechanical room.

Throughout the tour, as we peeked into offices and explored the stacks, I kept thinking to myself, *I can't believe I finally get to work here!*

After the tour, the remainder of my day was spent shadowing my new colleagues at the reference desk.

I remember the one thing that intimidated me the most was the shelf of "ready reference" resources behind the desk. Directories, dictionaries, almanacs, binders filled with financial data—I thought I was going to have to know every single volume and thus would fail miserably when it came to helping patrons find basic information.

Fortunately, I was paired with a veteran reference assistant with a folder of handouts and a two-week orientation that would prepare me for most situations. On my second day, I was introduced to a fellow library assistant who took the responsibility of training new hires seriously. Phone instruction, desk shadowing, catalog searching, and policy and procedure reading—it was intense.

I admittedly may not have appreciated it at the time, but this slightly over the top, yet thorough orientation ensured I had the skills and tools to serve the public. A tad overconfident in my abilities and eager to hit the ground running, I grew impatient while I was guided through the basic training.

"If it's an internal call, the ring will come in short blasts," the training assistant says. We're seated at one of the four desks squeezed into the small Adult Services office shared among five full-time and six part-time reference staff and the adult services coordinator.

"Here, listen as I call from the interlibrary loan line."

Are we seriously going over ring tones? I stare at the phone and listen to the ring. I'd never used a multi-line phone before, and I appreciated learning how to switch lines and transfer calls, but my patience is starting to run thin.

"If it's an external call, the ring blasts will be more sustained."

What does it matter if it's an internal or external call? I'm going to answer it anyway…

"When you're working in the back office, it's important to listen to the different ring tones," she continues. "The reference desk answers all external calls, but if they're busy and don't pick up before the fourth tone, the line will ring here in the office. If it's an external call that's transferred from another internal line…"

As it turns out, that information was helpful in the long run. Not that I made a habit of ignoring phone calls, but it was nice to know beforehand whether it was a patron calling or a coworker at the desk wanting a break.

Shadowing at the desk was my favorite part of orientation. On the library's main level, the reference desk was situated in the middle of the adult collections and was typically staffed by two reference assistants or librarians. We also staffed the desk on the lower level, where we provided tech support for the public computer lab.

Not only did I learn where everything was located and what tools to use to answer questions, but shadowing also provided the perfect opportunity to get to know regular patrons and their behaviors without having to interact with them directly. The coworkers I observed had tips for who typically asks for what, who comes in when, and who might be more likely to get angry or easily upset.

I found it interesting how different staff handled similar questions. Some were more likely to use the print resources behind the reference desk, while others relied more heavily on the Internet. I came to use the latter method more often myself, but there were times when the best and quickest way to find an answer was picking up one of the reverse directories, celebrity address books, or financial resources.

Those first two weeks of orientation also disproved some of the preconceived notions about working in libraries that I had accumulated over the years. First, for example, you don't *have* to know everything off the top of your head.

Even into my second semester of library school, I clung to the image of Forney Hull shuffling into the stacks and knowing the exact location of a book to answer one of Novalee's questions. It didn't take long for me to learn that I didn't have to have every book on the shelf memorized, but that I did need to know the tools that would help me find the ones I needed. Off-hand knowledge like Forney's is built up over years of working with a collection. My supervisor and (most) patrons didn't expect that of me. That's what the library catalog, coworkers, and, yes, even notorious Internet search engines are for.

Second: You *don't* get paid to sit and read all day. Mostly.

How do librarians become so familiar with their collections? How do they know what books to recommend? By reading on the job, of course. Or that's what I assumed. But nope. Not on the clock. Again, through years of working with the collection, skimming book reviews, and using the tools at our disposal, like readers' advisory databases, librarians become skilled at understanding the collection and making recommendations. If you happen to be a voracious reader on your own time, it helps.

Third: You don't *have* to have a master's degree to work at the library.

In my graduate school entrance interview, I told the program director that I was interested in working at the Lawrence Public Library. Familiar with the town and the library, she scared me and said that I would pretty much need a doctorate. However, after I did get a position without, in fact, having a doctorate or even my master's yet, I realized it was more of a statement of how hard it is to stand out among a large number of students who apply for the entry-level positions. As I got to know the staff, I was a little surprised to learn that not everyone who worked at the library had or wanted a master's degree.

Finally: Just because it's your dream job, doesn't mean you'll like everything about it.

Because a part of me felt like librarianship was my calling, I thought I was going to be happy every single day. For the most part, I did enjoy what I was doing, but there were still tasks that I didn't care for, there were still patrons who could ruin my whole day, and there were still coworkers I wanted to avoid. However, all that wasn't going to scare me away. I've always believed the negatives help you appreciate the things you do like about your job more.

Once I settled into my position, I wanted to do everything. I told myself never to say no to a task asked of me, no matter how tedious. From keeping track of reference desk statistics to shifting ranges full of books to sitting at the lower level computer lab service desk for more than two hours, I never hesitated to do things some of my coworkers deemed undesirable.

I knew immediately I had to have a full-time position and told Lynn I'd have to find somewhere else if I couldn't get one at LPL. After six long months, an opportunity presented itself. A coworker took maternity leave, and Lynn asked me to cover her responsibilities, checking in newspapers and magazines and helping process interlibrary loans.

When the coworker decided not to come back, her position was posted in-house. The original job was half serials work and half interlibrary loan, but Lynn chose to reconfigure the position to half serials and half reference. It wasn't exactly what I wanted to do, but I knew full-time opportunities were scarce, so I applied, interviewed, and got it!

Within another six months, as staff in other departments retired or left, more restructuring took place. The serials responsibilities that I had taken over were then given to the technical services department. Since I had finished my master's degree at that point, Lynn worked with the administration to give me the official, professional title of Reference Librarian, along with all the benefits that come with it. This finally gave me the time and freedom to do what I wanted.

By the end of my first stint at LPL, I was managing the library's Book Club in a Bag service, scheduling and teaching computer classes, providing technical support for eReaders, helping manage the library's social media accounts, creating readers' advisory handouts, putting together displays, planning programs, weeding a part of the collection, and serving on the staff development committee.

This well-rounded experience, combined with my passion for the work, prepared me for my next problem-filled adventure: serving as director of the Oskaloosa Public Library. But I'll get into all that shortly.

Part II:
Tales from...

Chapter 5
Circulation

One that happened to me today: When you open a returned DVD and a waft of marijuana smell hits your nostrils...and when the patron who returned that DVD spends 45 minutes wandering the DVD section bringing two things up to the circ desk at a time... Yeah bro, you high.

— Tumblr message

The circulation department. Some librarians might say this is where all the magic happens. Circulation staff meet and register new patrons, witness the joy as children check out stacks of their favorite books and movies, and help troubleshoot issues with accounts. They also get to endure arguments about small fines, listen to excuses for late returns, and handle items that are sopping wet, chewed up, or filled with pests.

Many librarians and library workers get their start in circulation as a library page. This entry-level position is generally responsible for making sure items are returned to their proper locations on the shelves. Other duties include emptying book drops, sorting and checking in items, retrieving reserves, and, the most thrilling of all, shelf reading.

You might think it a low-stress position. What could be so bad about shelving books all day? However, library pages see their fair share of problems. To a well-trained and passionate shelver, nothing is more frustrating than finding an entire section of books in disarray or shoved to the back of the shelves. To the impatient one, nothing irritates them more than trying to return a book to a shelf that a patron is browsing at a glacial pace.

I never officially held the page position, but when I returned to the Lawrence Public Library as a part-time readers' services assistant, shelving became one of my primary responsibilities in my new role. The page position had been eliminated in a reorganization of staff after the expansion and renovation, and librarians and library assistants in front-line departments were given more hands-on care of the collections they managed and promoted. Readers' Services, a brand-new department, handled the fiction and genre collections.

It was like I had come full circle in my library career, having served three years as a director, now shelving books and doing every page's favorite task: shelf reading. If you've ever spent a couple of hours shuffling slowly through the stacks reading spine labels and checking for things out of place, you know what I'm talking about. It's usually the last resort to "keep busy" when there's no shelving or anything else to be done.

My biggest pet peeve, though, was when someone would walk up behind me and start browsing the shelves above my head while I was shelving books on a bottom shelf. Now I never expected harm from patrons, but I always pictured the scene in horror movies where the killers or monsters or demons sneak up behind unsuspecting protagonists. I'd finish what I was doing as quickly as possible and get out of there.

Not today, demon!

Excuses, Excuses, Excuses

A patron came in with some books that were about 4 weeks overdue. His excuse: he was Anwar Sadat's wife's bodyguard and had been held over in Egypt

when Sadat was assassinated. I waived the fines. If
he was lying, he deserved to be awarded for excellent
imagination.

— Facebook comment

Desk clerks, typically the next step up from pages,
staff the circulation desk, check out items (if the
library hasn't moved to a primarily self-check model),
issue new library cards, and resolve problems with
patron accounts. I've never envied the job of circulation desk clerks, or their supervisors, as they bear
the brunt of patron account issues and hear a lot of
excuses for late, lost, or damaged items.

"I didn't know it was due then. Why didn't I get
an email notice?"

"I've never heard of that book. I wouldn't borrow something like that!"

"It was like that when I checked it out!"

They hear it all. Most of the time, library staff
will give the benefit of the doubt, especially for first-
time occurrences. We know life happens. But we're
also clever enough to realize when patrons are taking advantage of us. Insider tip: at most libraries,
staff will note in your account in the database when
you report a lost or stolen item. If it happens repeatedly, we know something's up.

As director at the Oskaloosa Library, I was often
called to the circulation desk to resolve issues with
accounts. One patron—I'll call her Sally—had a

wealth of stories and excuses to get out of being fined or billed for lost items. Things my staff knew she borrowed would go long-overdue, and when they would confront her about it, her common response was something along the lines of, "I've never heard of those. I don't read books like that. I wouldn't have checked those out."

I admit, she fooled me the first time.

The second time, I tried to confront her.

"Sally, I was told you have a few items on your account that are a week overdue," I said. "Do you know where those are?"

"I told that lady I never checked those books out," she responded.

"Are you sure? We've looked a few times and they're not on our shelves."

"Are you calling in me a liar?"

"No Sally, I wouldn't do that," I responded. I usually don't do well with confrontation and had to think quickly. "It's been a while since you checked them out. Could you have misplaced them?"

"I'm not a forgetful person, William."

"Well, what I'd like to do is leave them on your account for now, but extend the due dates," I said. I knew I was taking a gamble here. "Just to give you a couple more weeks to see if you find them."

"Fine. Whatever. I'll look, but I know I turned them in."

The items in question were in the book drop the next day.

As I got to know Sally, her excuses escalated from "I put those in the drop yesterday!" to "I gave those to my grandson to return. I'm positive he would have brought them in." to "My apartment was broken into. I think they stole those DVDs."

Each time I had to confront her, I felt like I was walking on eggshells. Whether she was lying compulsively, had trouble remembering, or honestly had the worst luck, I didn't want to offend her. I pledged not to make a blanket assumption about her, to consider each situation individually, and to work with her to see if we could get items back to the library. Even though she was a trying patron, she still had every right to use the library and have a positive experience.

Patrons like Sally make me appreciate and admire the work of circulation desk clerks and their supervisors. I'm no longer in a position where I get to resolve these issues, but I still feel their pain. Dealing with these kinds of interactions regularly leaves its mark on you!

The Problem with Overdue Fines

I once had a patron checkout 50 Disney DVDs across about 6 cards (all family members) for their upcoming trip to Disneyworld. So they come back and

have upwards of $150 in fines across all the cards.
They tried to blame it on a hurricane—a hurricane
that hit three days after they got home from their trip!

— Facebook comment

In libraries that still charge overdue fees, circulation staff might agree that they're the number-one cause of contention with patrons. Sometimes even the smallest fine can instigate the angriest response if the patron swears that they turned it in on time or shouldn't be fined because they weren't notified that the item was due.

Another time in Oskaloosa, I was called down from my office to find a disgruntled parent, arms crossed and a scowl on his face. From a phone in the back, one of the library assistants told me they had already gotten into it with him about an overdue book.

"Hi, I'm William," I said. "I was told there's a problem with your account?"

"Yeah, my daughter was fined for a book." He took a step toward me. "What's the deal with this?"

"Let me take a look at her account," I responded. "Can you tell me what the book was?"

"No," he shouted. "You need to fix this now."

"Okay," I said. This happened to be my first interaction with a patron upset with overdue fines. I felt like a mouse confronting a lion. I could feel my pulse rising and hands starting to shake, but I tried my best to maintain a calm demeanor. The circulation desk was in proximity to the children's area, and I didn't want to escalate the situation around other patrons.

"I need to look at her account, though. Would you mind if we go to my office? We can figure this out there."

He sighed, nodded, and followed me up the stairs. When I brought up his daughter's account on my computer, I saw that she had an overdue book that had started accumulating fines. They couldn't renew it because there was a hold on it for another patron.

"My daughter needs this book to finish a school assignment," he explained to me. "Why are we being billed for this? It's not right."

In his mind, he and his daughter were being punished because the library didn't have another copy of the book. We should have known about the demand for the book because of the school assignment.

"I understand why you feel like you're being punished," I said. "And I apologize that we don't have another copy of the book. If you'll let me, I'd like to explain our system here and see what we can do to help you."

Having not thought about the inequity of overdue fines, I suggested he think of the charges as convenience fees. I explained that the library board had set what they agreed was a fair amount of time for patrons to borrow items. If someone wanted or needed more time with the item that another patron was waiting for, they could pay a small fee to have the convenience of keeping that item longer.

"I guess that's fair," he said, "but that still doesn't help my daughter. We need the book longer."

"What I'll do this time is forgive the fine and extend the due date a week," I said. "Do you think that'll be enough time for her to finish the project?"

"Yeah, I think so," he said.

While spinning overdue fines as convenience fees may have de-escalated this situation, I realize now how problematic that was. This situation happened a few years before a national trend of library leaders thinking critically about the practice of charging overdue fines, but I now know I could have thought better about what I had suggested.

Recently, several libraries and library systems have acknowledged that overdue fees are an inequitable barrier to access. In a 2019 "Resolution on Monetary Library Fines as a Form of Social Inequity," the American Library Association urged "libraries to scrutinize their practices of imposing fines on library patrons and actively move towards eliminating them." That year several large systems, including the Chicago Public Library, the Kansas City (Missouri) Public Library, and the Seattle Public Library, went or pledged to go fine-free.

The ALA and these systems have recognized that this method of holding patrons accountable prevents people, especially those living at or below the poverty level, from using the library. If access to information and resources is a library's core value, sustaining a punitive system for holding items past a due date works against that value, as it becomes a barrier for those who, for whatever reason, cannot afford to pay those fines.

Suggesting that patrons could pay for the convenience of having items longer was an exacerbation of that inequity on my part, and I regret, now, having spun it that way. I'm not sure where the Oskaloosa Library is in their understanding of overdue fines today, but I know if I were still there, I'd make the case to eradicate them.

Strange Things Found in Book Drops

Now for the really heavy discussion: the chore of emptying book drops.

Seriously, depending on the size of the library and how busy it is, emptying a book drop can sometimes be an exhausting, stressful, and even dangerous task.

Ever try to load as many items in your arms to make as few trips as possible? Ever have a thousand-page hardcover nearly smack you in the head? Ever wait for a hoard of children to drop one book at a time into the return slot? Ever find a dead bird smashed beneath a pile of books?

Yes, it's happened, but that's not the wildest thing discovered in a drop. On the *Librarian Problems* Facebook page, I asked what the strangest thing librarians have found while retrieving returned materials at their libraries. Here are a few of the weirdest:

> *I opened one morning to be greeted by a squirrel who had gotten in there and gotten stuck. He was nice enough to not pop out at me until after I had opened it and dragged out the cart, but still gave me a heart attack.*

> *A stolen license plate from a car. It happened while we were closed for Thanksgiving. Came in on Saturday morning and there it was on top of the pile. Screws still attached and everything.*

> *Remains of a fried chicken leg, DVD cases filled with live cockroaches, and acid poured into the drop on all the books.*

A hot dog. No bun, no plate, like maybe someone thought it was a trash can. Just an uncooked hot dog.

A box of those Good Choice chickpea crackers under a load of books. Box was still pristine and totally unopened. Baffles me.

A kitten. He was physically fine and now lives with a staff member and is only a little crazy, but who can blame him!

I was emptying the book drop when I heard a car pull up outside, so I stepped back and waited for their returns to drop in. Several books and DVDs came down the chute, then a pause, then... a full bag of Taco Bell, still warm & the top folded up tight.

A pointy piece of a wrought iron fence. A patron popped up behind me and said, 'Oh, that's my spear.' and grabbed it out of my hand. An argument ensued over whether it was a weapon and if he could bring it in the library.

A blood-bathed book. A patron's grandmother had hemorrhaged and died while reading it and the granddaughter threw it in the book drop. Luckily, it was empty at the time...

We found a female contraceptive device and my boss didn't realize what it was and kept picking it up asking people if they lost it when they came into the library. I explained it wasn't what he thought it was and we needed to get rid of it and sanitize the counter.

My coworker had a mouse pop out at her once! She screamed and flailed across the parking lot; we caught it on our security cameras!

In Indiana, the police were called because someone reported that a person was stuffing a dead cat in the book drop. It turned out to be a mom, returning a puppet she had borrowed.

A beautifully written letter tucked inside a book that was from the borrower to the next reader describing how this book touched her life (she was an older widow and felt that books were helping keep her happy). We put the letter back inside the book.

Chapter 6
Reference

I had someone drop two large, living, wet, sandy bivalves on my desk and demand to know what they were. While I researched the creatures, he proceeded to the restroom with a 5-gallon bucket of them and cleaned them all. For the record, they were enormous Great Atlantic Scallops.

— *Facebook comment*

Because I got my start in Reference, it will always hold a special place in my heart. And because some of my wildest library experiences happened while at the reference desk, my time there will forever be seared into my memory.

Like the evening shift when a patron approached the desk, a sour expression on her face, to report that there was "a mess" in the elevator (I won't go into details here). Fortunately, there was a maintenance staff member still on the clock who simply ripped up and disposed of the carpet square, mess and all.

There's also the time that I had to call 911 because an elderly man had collapsed in the periodicals section in a full-on seizure. Unfortunately, I'm one of those types that tend to freeze up at the sight of a life-threatening situation, but thanks to the prompting of a helpful bystander, I dialed the emergency number. By the time the paramedics arrived, the gentleman's seizure had ended, and they assured my coworkers and me that he would recover.

Not all my experiences on the reference desk were negative. While most memorable, the wild, unexpected situations were rare. It was the day to day tasks mixed in with these exceptional times that helped me appreciate my work the most.

Reference staff get to help patrons find materials, solve problems, and learn new things. They get to chat about books, connect people with resources, and build relationships. I'd say the best part of the job, though, is the wide range of questions you get to help answer. From quick ones like "Can you give me the phone number to Walgreens?" to in-depth research like "I'm writing a paper on the history of the Osage and Pawnee peoples in Kansas. Can you help me find resources?" you never know what you're going to get, and that makes each day interesting.

One of my favorite questions at the Lawrence Library came over the phone from what I assumed was a child making a serious inquiry...or a teenager playing a prank. Back then, reference staff answered external calls at the desk on the public floor.

"Lawrence Public Library reference," I answered one afternoon. "How can I help you?"

"Hi Lawrence Public Library reference!" the caller said in a sing-song voice.

"Hello. How can I help you?" I repeated.

"Do you have turtles?"

"No, I'm sorry," I said.

"Aww," they whined.

"We have books about turtles, though," I said.

"But I want turtles!"

"I'm sorry," I responded. "But you'll have to..."

They hung up before I could finish. Clearly, our lack of turtles was a problem.

One of the library assistants at the Oskaloosa Library told me about a fun question she received over the phone once too. When she answered the call, she also wasn't sure it was a serious inquiry.

"What color should I paint my fairy?" the caller asked.

This one was real. The caller had purchased a ceramic fairy at a craft show and wasn't sure what color to paint it, so she decided to call the library for advice.

"I had to put the phone down for a second because I was so tickled," the library assistant said when sharing the story with me. "Then I did a Google search for fairies and described some of the images I found. A lot of pinks, blues, yellows, and pastels, I told her."

While most of the questions we get at the desk are a bit more serious, it's often the fun ones like these that make our days. Here are some of the best reference questions shared on the *Librarian Problems* Facebook page:

"Are these books arranged in any particular order?"

From a kid: "Do you go home at night?" (He wanted to sleep at the library and didn't believe his mother when she told him the staff don't live there.)
"Can you move the trees on google earth so I can see the fence in my back yard?"

A customer once asked me for a book on Nova Scotia. I'd taken her to the section for countries and travel, she looked for a while and said that wasn't what she wanted. "You know who I mean," she said, "Nova Scotia, that bloke who did all the predictions!" She meant Nostradamus!

"Do you fart?" by a little girl who was checking out a book on farts.

A phone call at the library: "What are the lyrics to the original Scooby-Doo theme song?" Their internet was down so I couldn't email them, had to recite them over the phone.

A little old lady came in and asked my director to baby-sit a can of beans while she browsed. Yep, a can of beans. She was very insistent, and my director finally said yes, taking the beans with her whenever she had to leave the desk. The old lady ended up leaving without them.

Guy came in with a framed photo of Pope John Paul II. Behind that photo was a picture of a young couple, wearing 70s fashions. The patron wanted to know if he was holding concrete proof that the Pope had been married.

Did we have any materials on exorcism or how to cleanse a home of ghosts? The same patron also wanted

me to look "in the book" and tell her who died in her
house in the past.

Lending an Ear

Whether we like it or not, librarians are like bartenders for the daytime—a captive audience behind a counter or desk ready to listen to your gossip, your problems, your family histories, your current obsessions, or whatever else comes to mind. Reference librarians, specifically, are prime targets for those in need of human connection, because, unlike the circulation desk, things tend to be slower paced in our neck of the library.

It can be a bit of a conundrum. While we want to provide a positive experience for all patrons, we also need to be ready and available to help those who have information needs. Some patrons will wait their turn, or for the librarian to kindly interrupt the chatter, but others tend to avoid approaching the desk if they perceive an in-depth conversation taking place.

Who do you prioritize? The patron recounting a recent trip to the podiatrist? Or the person who walks up behind them who might need help finding a book?

For those who are "too nice," it's even more of a struggle when no one else is waiting. I've heard from librarians who've devised a solution for such situations. If a conversation reaches a certain point, they'll somehow signal to their coworkers who will then call from an office or approach the reference desk. "I'm sorry to interrupt, but you've got a phone call in the back" makes for an easy getaway.

I intend no shame here. Sometimes librarians are the only human connection a patron might get in their day. And you never know what fascinating information you might learn or stories you might hear.

Agatha (pseudonym), a regular at the Oskaloosa Library, was famous for occupying up to thirty minutes of staff time recounting tales and chatting at the reference desk. An elderly woman, who my staff knew well, lived with a questionable number of cats. She would often visit the library with the intent to post lengthy handwritten diatribes against the city's animal control, who she believed was unfairly targeting her.

She would visit at least once a week, and I'd often encounter her deep in conversation with whoever was stationed at the reference desk. Wrapped in a faded overcoat and hand-knit scarves, she would perch on the edge of a chair across from the desk, lean on her cane, and launch into a string of tangentially related stories connected with "Oh, and…"

One day, she had a library assistant call me out of my office. Hoping we didn't do something to upset her, I found her in the usual spot and greeted her.

"Oh, hello William," she said. "I wanted to thank you for posting my note. It's hard for me to get around these days, and people need to know what the city is up to…"

I could barely get a word in edgewise to say, "You're welcome."

"Honestly, they can't come on to my property and go after my cats. I'm taking care of them the best I know how. Who do they think they are?"

When she finished ranting about animal control, she moved on to a completely different topic. "Oh, and did I tell you that I worked for Macy's marketing department? They flew me all over the place. When I stayed in Colorado, I met…"

I listened for about five minutes as she casually dropped names, claiming to have met celebrities and wealthy politicians, and recounted road trips and flights. When I glanced around for a chair to pull over, she must have thought I was looking for an out.

"I don't want to take more of your time," she said, rising from her seat.

"It's okay," I said. "I don't mind."

She then sat back down and began again with, "Oh, and did I mention that…"

I tried not to sigh…or laugh.

Tax Season (*dun dun dun!*)

They come in January. If they're on time, that is.

For some, the New Year brings the excitement of new beginnings and fresh starts. Reference librarians, though, are subject to the cyclical nature of time, and to us, the first of January means another round of tax season, and another round of tax season means tax forms and instruction booklets. *Dun dun dun!*

The main headache of tax season is having to field the same question from multiple, if not dozens, of people a day. "Do you have/Where are the tax forms?"

You might be thinking, *What's the big deal? If you didn't want to help people find tax forms, why work at a library?*

And you'd be right. It's not a big deal. And we're always more than willing to show patrons where they are. But when you start getting these questions as early as, say, November (or even October!), and you know you're going to get them through the best part of April, they kind of start getting to you.

Generally, the intensity of a patron's request for forms is directly proportional to their eagerness to get their taxes completed and behind them. Now consider when—*dun dun dun!*—legislators decide to make last-minute changes to tax laws, pushing the release of forms to the end of January...or even into February.

When I first started at the Lawrence Library, boxes and boxes of instruction booklets and various forms would arrive anytime from mid to late January. One lucky reference librarian would get the joy of sorting and arranging them on a large rotating display stand placed strategically next to signage that read "Tax forms" in all caps.

It never failed. No matter how clear that signage was, no matter where it was placed, many patrons would walk right past it and ask where the tax forms were. The words could have been in flashing neon lights, and I bet we'd still get questions at the desk.

As disparaging as this may sound, I do mean this as more of an observation than a criticism. Sometimes a simple directional question is the starting point for more in-depth information needs; sometimes people, for whatever reason, can't perceive or read signage, and sometimes people just prefer human interaction. I'm not judging anyone for that.

In the years since my first reference job, revenue offices began printing and sending fewer and fewer forms and encouraging the public to file their taxes electronically. The Kansas Department of Revenue, for example, quit supplying printed forms to libraries and public places altogether, and now only send forms to individuals by request.

While we have fewer forms to sort through, this has only served to further complicate tax season for libraries. Those yet to embrace, understand, or even trust the Internet continue to come to the library for printed instruction booklets and forms. Now librarians are either assisting non-digital natives in accessing and printing forms, or we're explaining, repeatedly, that we don't receive certain ones anymore, but you can call some state department number and hopefully get a response.

Once we get them to the forms, the fun doesn't always stop there. Often, we'll then get the most dreaded tax-related question of all: "Which form should I use?"

Dun dun dun!

As simple as it seems, most public librarians are not in the position to answer this question because of liability. We aren't trained in tax law, and we don't want to be responsible for leading patrons in the wrong direction. While some libraries do offer tax assistance programs, they're most likely led by certified advisors or tax preparers.

We're more than happy, though, to ~~pass you off~~ direct you to other resources and services in the community.

The Fun of Mis-heard Titles

Sometimes patrons honestly ask for the impossible. And by impossible, I mean they ask for books that don't exist. They'll hear about a novel from a friend or a radio program, or read about it in a newspaper or magazine, fail to jot the title down, and try to dredge it from their memories when they get to the library. Sometimes they get close enough that librarians can suss out the actual book that they want. Shared on the *Librarian Problems* Facebook page:

> *A patron called to ask if we had "The Fast and the Furious," the new book about Donald Trump. She was looking for Fire and Fury by Michael Wolff.*

> *"The Torso Ranch" by Pat Cornwall. Just started to type that when I realized. "Do you mean The Body Farm by Patricia Cornwell?" Yep.*

> *Students ask for "How to Kill a Mockingbird." Now, when we checkout Harper Lee's book, I just call it "How to Kill a Mockingjay."*

Got asked for "The Grape Giraffe" once…otherwise known as The Grapes of Wrath.

Other times, the book is so far off base it takes a little bit more digging. We'll usually ask for an author, a summary of the plot, or a description of the cover. If that doesn't work, we'll try to dig up the article or radio program. We don't give up easily.

I had an elderly patron ask for the movie "Hidden Fingers." She held up her fingers and wiggled them so I know I didn't misunderstand.

I had a customer ask for a book their professor told them to get called "Tease" by Tim McGraw. What they really wanted was the TEAS Review book by McGraw-Hill.

"The diarrhea books." I went for the "Wimpy Kid" books first, then found she wanted the "Dork Diaries." But oh how I wanted to laugh.

Patron needed a book for her daughter. The title was "something, something after dawn." It took a while, but I figured out she wanted "Flowers for Algernon."

"The Genius Book. It's for the world's smartest people." Oh, you mean the one with things like world's longest fingernails? *"Yup, that's it."*

And sometimes, it's the librarian who mishears the title:

I was the one who misheard a title over the phone. The patron wanted The Courage to Heal and I heard "The Carriage to Hell." Luckily the patron had a sense of humor.

I'm guilty of this too. One day when I was working the reference desk at the Lawrence Library, a guy approached and asked for what I thought was *48 Ways to Work Your Love.*

Now that sounds like a hot read, I thought to myself. After searching the library's catalog and coming up with nothing, though, I switched over to Google. No exact results. I got the feeling I misheard the title but didn't want to admit it.

"I'm not finding that," I said. "Could you tell me who the author is?"

"Miller, I think," he responded. "Dan Miller."

I typed that into Google and blushed, realizing what happened. When I switched back to the library's catalog, I typed in *48 Days to the Work You Love*.

I'd like to blame the discrepancy on my being hard of hearing, but I must be honest. I might have been a little flustered by the attractive patron. Hey, it happens!

Chapter 7

Youth Services

Two-year-old discovered hidden zipper on a yellow beanbag chair. While we were distracted, doing crafts for the preschoolers, he opened it up and spread the contents all over the children's department. It looked like snow.... At least he didn't eat any of it.

— Facebook comment

I'll be honest here. I've never really thought working in Youth Services was for me. Not because I hate youth, but because children's rooms and teen zones can be chaos. Teens gossiping and messing around on their phones, kids playing video games and shouting, toddlers giggling and ransacking the shelves, babies wailing...

Okay, okay. It's not always the nightmare I'm making it out to be, but I seriously believe youth services librarians and assistants should be commended for their patience, their creativity, and their ability to enrapture a room full of wiggling toddlers with storytime or ~~coerce~~ encourage a group of tweens and teens to participate in "lame" activities.

Whether it's in the stacks, gathered around a storytime theater, or about town on outreach visits, youth services librarians experience some of the wildest and funniest encounters with their young patrons. Here are some of my favorite moments shared on the *Librarian Problems* Facebook page:

I once did a storytime with a "treasure hunt" for some in-the-shell peanuts. When I brought the kids out of the storytime room and into the library to look for the peanuts, an adult was sitting at one of the tables reading the paper. There was a big pile of peanut shells on the table.

One of our regular little guys turned to me at the end of a song and said, "Miss Laura, maybe you shouldn't try to sing anymore. You're really not good."

A kindergartener pulled out a switchblade to help me out when sharing a story about the contents of a boy's pockets coming to life.

When I was pregnant...the group asked me how the baby was going to come out. I told them very calmly that when it was ready, I would go to the hospital and the Dr. would take it out. I had a little girl stand up and say, "That's not how it works...you will shoot the baby out of your vagina."

At a kinder visit doing a dads theme for Father's Day, a little girl very sadly told me she didn't have a daddy because he was dead. The kinder teacher came over and said "Your daddy is not dead. He dropped you off this morning!"

I was reading "Count the Monkeys" at a school visit to a kindergarten. When I got to the part where there are 9 lumberjacks, but still no monkeys a little boy yelled in a very exasperated voice, "Oh, Jesus Christ!"

I was reading a book about a ladybug and a real ladybug flew in and landed on me. The kids thought I was a wizard.

I was reading a book with a dog in it. I wanted to engage so I said: "Does anyone have a dog at home?" This little girl, whom I will never forget, said in the most Wednesday Addams way ever, "My dog is dead. My dad buried him in the yard."

I was at the Summer Reading points desk when a little 6-year-old came up with a big picture book: "My brother [did something unmentionable to] this, can I still get points?" I held up the trash can and said, "Of course you can sweetie, put it right in here for me."

"You're not the library lady!"

When the longtime children's librarian at Oskaloosa submitted her retirement notice, I began shadowing her to get an idea of the scope of her job. I didn't want there to be a disruption in service while we searched for someone to fill the position and was planning to cover things myself in the interim in case other staff didn't like the idea.

As a one-person children's department, she covered the desks, ordered books for the collection, and planned and presented storytimes for preschoolers, after-school programs for older kids, and monthly events for teens. She also spent a significant amount of time visiting and delivering books to preschool and elementary classrooms.

"I'm glad you're taking the time to come along with me, William," she said to me when I accompanied her on one of the school visits. "You'll see just how important it is that someone read to these kids."

I followed her as she tugged a mobile crate full of books along the sidewalk and into the elementary school. She stopped to consult her handwritten schedule, and then we made our way through the hallways to the first classroom.

"It's the library lady!" a kindergartener exclaimed when she peeked her head into the open door.

"Shhhhh," the children's librarian shushed with a grin. But it was too late. The class, excited for the visit, erupted with gasps and greetings, and the teacher invited us in.

Watching her engage with the children was magical. They listened as she read stories, sang along with her, and giggled and laughed as she performed with a monkey puppet named George. I knew then that the kids were going to miss her, and whoever I found to fill the position would have a big job ahead of them.

When her last day came and went, I found myself covering storytimes because, as I had guessed, no other staff took me up on the offer when I asked if they'd like the opportunity. I'm sad to say, the magic was lacking.

"Hi everyone!" I remember greeting a small group of preschoolers. "I'm Library Director William, and I'm going to be leading storytime for a couple of weeks."

The kids stared with their wide, unblinking eyes. I couldn't tell if they were scared or confused or disappointed. A little girl started tearing up after I started to sing a gathering rhyme, and I paused when I noticed no one else was singing along.

"Won't you sing a song with me?"

"Where's George?" one of them asked.

"I'm sorry, George has retired," I admitted sadly.

Gasps.

I wasn't about to ruin George's memory by poorly imitating the retired librarian's performance. I could just imagine the toddlers running terrified from the room at the sound of my screeching interpretation.

As I got the hang of it, I came to enjoy sharing stories with the kids and singing rhymes and songs, and the regulars eventually warmed up to me. I got to be silly, and I loved getting babies and toddlers to giggle and smile. However, it wasn't always grins and giggles. In my limited experience, I learned that there are three types of children that are the most trying during storytimes:

First, there are those who need a nap. Either they're cranky and interrupting stories or they're falling asleep on their little carpet squares or their parents' laps.

Then there are the kids who know everything and have "heard this story a thousand times!" They correct your pronunciation, they ruin picture books for others, and they laugh and point out your mistakes.

And finally, there are the kids who probably shouldn't be there in the first place. Why? Because they're sick. I've fortunately never had a toddler blow snot bubbles on me or throw up during a silly dance, but I've heard the horror stories. Regardless of how temperamental some kids could be, I always walked away with a smile.

My favorite thing that happened during a story-time caught me completely off guard. The holidays were approaching, and I chose to read a book about reindeer. To introduce the book, I asked, "Does anyone know what a reindeer is?"

Before I could call on the few kids who raised their hands, a little boy shouted, "You shoot them and eat them!"

I was so shocked, I couldn't respond. A parent sitting in on the program covered her mouth and silently laughed. Thankfully, another kid spoke up and said something about the North Pole and Santa.

"Very good!" I said, trying to keep a straight face. "Today I'm going to share a story all about the reindeer."

When I later shared about this on Facebook, a friend pointed out that I set myself up for this one. Asking about deer in rural Iowa? I shouldn't have been surprised.

While I had a lot of fun with it, covering in the absence of the children's librarian helped me realize that leading storytime takes time, talent, and practice and isn't for everyone. Especially me. Who honestly wants to hear me croak out an attempt at "Mmm, Ahh Went the Little Green Frog"? Fortunately, it wasn't my full-time gig, and a newly hired children's librarian stepped into the role shortly thereafter.

The True Test of Children's Librarianship

Fresh out of library school, Liz accepted the children's librarian position and moved to Oskaloosa in the middle of January. I'm not sure if I effectively communicated the extent of the responsibilities or the size of the shoes she'd be filling after someone who'd worked in the position for thirty years, but she hit the ground running, planning storytimes and after school programs, managing the children's collection, and making the position her own.

Starting in January, though, meant that she immediately had to start thinking about summer reading, the true test of children's librarianship. Intended to engage children and encourage reading during the two and a half months most kids would be out of school, a successful summer reading program can take up to four months to plan.

Against the better judgment of staff who'd been through it before, Liz and I made some lofty goals that first year. Wanting to engage children the entire summer, we extended the normal six-week program to nine. We also planned to expand the teen and adult programs with events and reading challenges specifically geared to those age groups.

In addition to regular storytimes for preschoolers and babies, Liz scheduled weekly afternoon events for older kids. Puppeteers, clowns, magicians, musicians, and animal keepers—she got a head start booking performers and putting together crafts, outdoor games, and other activities. She also worked closely with one of the library assistants, who normally helped by designing posters and flyers to promote the program and events.

It would all begin with a kickoff party in the library's reading garden. That year's theme was "Dig into Reading," so Liz and the library assistant prepared seed planting and treasure digging activities. Veteran staff warned us that kickoff parties were typically the biggest event of the year. This one was no exception.

The weather on that early June afternoon couldn't have been more perfect. We set up the activity stations in the garden under a cloudless blue sky, stocked the children's reference desk with hundreds of reading logs and registration slips, and popped corn in a popper we borrowed from a nearby bank. Then we sat back and waited for the fun to begin.

I had yet to see the library so crowded! The parents and children came in hordes to register for the program, check out books, and enjoy the activities and free popcorn. Over two hundred kids signed up, and the staff checked out over 1,274 items that day alone. As impressive as I believed that was for our small library, it was a harbinger of what was to come.

Modeled after previous years, the reading challenge encouraged kids to read throughout the summer. For every book or block of time they read, they would earn summer reading dollars to spend on small prizes at the children's desk. Every child who participated was also entered into a grand prize drawing, which was announced at the end of the summer.

Liz and the rest of the staff at Oskaloosa impressed me that year with their hard work, patience, and collaboration. The weekly programs brought anywhere between twenty-five and fifty children, and before and after each, lines would form at the checkout counter and the children's desk. When I got the chance to cover one, I could barely keep up with the returns, checkouts, questions, account issues, new card registrations, and prize transactions. It made me appreciate what my staff did daily!

I've observed discussions among youth librarians on #LibraryTwitter about how exhausting and draining summers can be, especially when there's little to no support from other departments or administration. Increased programming means more children in the library, which means more questions at the desk, more items to check in and shelve, and sometimes more behavior issues to address. Who wouldn't experience burnout or at least be ready for a vacation after six to nine weeks of that?

Liz did an amazing job working with the rest of the staff at Oskaloosa and leading a successful program that year. While I'm sure she felt the pressure, I hope that she also felt supported in her role. She has since moved on to greater things, but I couldn't have hoped for a better youth librarian to fill the role.

Night of the Hungry Teens

Before Liz arrived, I made it a goal for the library to improve programming for teens in Oskaloosa. A core group of middle and high school-aged kids attended monthly teen advisory board (TAB) meetings and planned a few annual events, and that was the extent of programs for them. Recalling my negative experience at my hometown library when I was in middle school, I wanted to do better.

To me, services for teens are as important for encouraging life-long library users as any other age group, if not more. Many small libraries do well with children's programming but sometimes struggle with teen services. If we're able to tempt them into the library with a welcoming and engaging program, though, it's easier for them to see what else the library has to offer. After Liz joined the library staff and took over the children's storytimes, I figured I could help us do more with the teens.

Summer provided our first opportunity to go beyond the TAB meetings. With teens' suggestions, we offered chess club, Dungeons & Dragons, messy games, and crafting programs. Used to only helping at younger children's programs, the teens were excited to have their own events. Because attendance was strong, we continued a few of the programs into the fall, splitting the planning and hosting responsibilities.

As October approached, we started working with the TAB to plan a special Halloween party. Figuring we'd have our dozen or so regulars, we kept it simple—snacks, a few activities, and a costume contest. I designed a flyer announcing the party, printed a small stack, and asked the TAB members to distribute them at school.

The afternoon before the party, we decorated the large meeting space on the third floor of the library with an odd arrangement of Halloween decorations we found in the library's storage. We made a tray of zombie and witch fingers (celery and cheese sticks), crafted spider suckers (Blow Pops with pipe cleaner legs), and set out bowls for chips, crackers, and candy. As the start time approached, we figured we'd see our regular teens, and it'd be a pretty calm, yet fun, evening. Boy were we wrong.

It was like *Night of the Living Dead.* The teens kept coming, and they were hungry. I swear, each youth that shuffled into the room was led by some preternatural urge to feed and went straight for the snacks. Fifteen minutes in, and almost all the food was consumed. I did a quick headcount and discovered we had more than forty teens! Most of them were milling about and picking at the devastated remnants of chips and candy.

I asked Liz to start one of the games and then dashed down the two flights of stairs to the children's programming room to rummage through the cupboards and gather anything edible onto a cart. Graham crackers, popcorn, juice boxes—there wasn't much. I returned, out of breath, and hastily laid out the offering before the activity concluded.

Where did all these teens come from? I wondered. I hadn't seen most of them in the library before, and it baffled me that they would suddenly show up to our meager party.

Because of our modest expectations, it was just the two of us newbie librarians against the horde. Despite our best efforts, we couldn't contain them. Several kept wandering in and out of the meeting room, running up and down the stairs, and out the front doors of the library. No amount of yelling "Please stay in the meeting room!" could convince them.

I felt sorry for the rest of the staff in the building who were woefully unprepared for the teenage invasion. When I took a moment to check in on them, tough, they just shrugged and laughed it off. If they could handle this, Liz and I can, I told myself.

The activities were somewhat a success. The younger teens giggled and laughed through the blindfolded face painting and mummy wrapping games while most of the older ones, more inclined to undead tendencies, rolled their eyes and groaned at the prospect of participating and wandered off again.

When we announced that the grand prize winner of the costume contest would receive a gift certificate to Somkey Row, a popular coffee shop and hangout, amazingly they reappeared. A number of them didn't bother dressing up, though, so among Doctor Who characters, superheroes, and monsters, the lineup featured several "teenagers" and last-minute adornments.

After all that, Liz and I were nearing the end of our energy reserves. We eventually gave up monitoring the food situation, figuring the empty bowls would encourage most to call it a night. As the clock crept toward the closing hour, the crowd slowly thinned, and then we ushered the few stragglers out the door.

"This was fun," a middle schooler dressed as Luigi said before leaving. "Thank you!"

Liz and I sighed and gazed over the room littered with popcorn kernels, chip crumbs, toilet paper, and empty cups. The "fun"—for us, at least—wasn't over yet.

Chapter 8
Tech Support

I had a patron who thought the whole staff was capable and actively hacking into his Yahoo account because he couldn't remember his password and didn't know the answers to his safety questions....because with the ability to hack, I would choose to work in a public library. Right.

— Facebook comment

Public libraries are one of the few places where people can access computers and the Internet for free or with no strings attached. Thus, tech support has become a significant job responsibility for librarians and library workers, specifically those who cover desks in computer labs. From the basics like signing on to a computer to the more in-depth like setting up an email account, staff help patrons with a wide variety of technology-related tasks.

If you've ever helped a parent or a relative with any sort of technology, you'll know that it takes a great deal of patience. Now imagine doing that multiple times a day, several days a week. You might find yourself wincing at the words "I forgot my password." Especially when they're followed with, "I don't remember answering these security questions!" and ultimately "Alternate email? I don't even know how to sign in to this one!"

Some of my coworkers dreaded shifts at the tech desk on the lower level of the pre-renovated Lawrence Library. Unlike the main reference desk that was staffed two at a time, you were on your own in a dimly lit space with twenty-four public access PCs, a genealogy collection, periodical back-issues, and nonfiction overflow. Some days you were troubleshooting printer issues, confronting patrons about headphone volume levels, setting up amateur genealogists on microfilm readers, finding books in the stacks, and more.

Lynn, the adult services coordinator and my supervisor, would try not to schedule anyone more than two hours at a time, but on the rare occasion, you got a shift that would last, it seemed, for days. Fear was not an option.

The interactions that tested my patience the most were helping patrons register or sign in to websites. We had one regular patron who swore up and down that the website she needed changed every time she tried to access it. My heart went out to her, though, because she came to the library weekly to apply for jobs and register for unemployment.

Each visit, she would pull a stack of wrinkled printouts and scrap papers from a tote bag, arrange them on the desktop, and then peck her thirteen-digit library card barcode into the keyboard one number at a time. If she managed to make it past the computer sign-on, it was a good day. If not, she would shuffle up to the desk insisting there was something wrong with the computer.

"Why do you guys make this so complicated?" she would grumble. "My computer isn't working. Please help me."

I would then follow her back to her computer and watch patiently as she tried typing in her number again. If she was successful, she would admit she probably mistyped a number. If not, it was the computer's fault. If I offered to try and was able to log her onto the desktop, it was still the computer's fault.

"Okay, it looks like you're good to go," I'd say. And knowing full well I'd likely be back at her side in a few minutes, "Let me know if you need more help."

Even though she, and other patrons, could get frustrated to tears, I always tried my best to exercise patience and understanding with them. Working the tech desk taught me that the availability of computers and Internet access in the library is vitally important to those who can't afford it, and the free assistance from trained library staff helps bridge that digital divide. I never wanted to scare away those who needed extra help.

Community Computer Classes

A few months after I started at Lawrence, the library received a grant to remodel a space on the lower level into a computer lab designed for teaching classes. The lab included twelve additional computers, a SMART Board, and an instructor station. Knowing I had technology skills and an interest in teaching, Lynn asked me to develop basic classes to offer to the public for free. Intro to Computers, Microsoft Word Basics, Internet 101—the classes were most suited for older adults with little to no experience using computers.

So, I went from doing tech help one-on-one to trying to help up to twelve people at once! It wasn't all bad, though. I loved the "ah-ha!" moments when participants finally understood how to open a program using a desktop icon, the excitement when they attached their first photo to an email, and their curiosity and fascination when completing Google searches.

My favorite classes to teach were about Facebook, even though the sessions typically left me scatter-brained and exhausted. With any of the computer classes, attendees' abilities varied, and a lot of the times I would need to pause to catch someone up or explain something again. When teaching people how to use Facebook, though, there's so much going on it's even harder to stay on topic.

During the first class I offered, I learned quickly that walking twelve people through Facebook's registration process at once isn't a good idea. The short registration form was easy enough, but it was the email confirmation that derailed the class. Most of the participants were able to login to their accounts, but some either didn't have an email account (even though the course description clearly stated one was needed) or didn't know their passwords.

After spending a good fifteen minutes trying to help these few participants recover their passwords, complicated by security questions and the dreaded captchas, I gave up and kindly asked them to observe. I realized then I should have had a teaching assistant.

From there, I covered the difference between the news feed and the profile timeline, how to post updates and photos, how to find friends to add and pages to like, and how to send private messages and chat with friends. I made sure to warn them, though, that every six to twelve months, Facebook likes to update, change and rearrange things, so they shouldn't get used to something being the same for too long.

By the time I got through all that, I looked at the clock and my hour was up.

No matter how much I prepared beforehand, every Facebook session was the same. I'd get to explaining one thing, and someone would have a question about something slightly related but just off-topic enough to get me on a tangent, and I'd end up feeling like I went in circles. All the while, most of the class would be scratching their heads.

What Kind of Computer Do You Use?

When I moved into my director position in Oskaloosa, I couldn't give up teaching tech skills. In addition to classes, I began offering one-on-one appointments, and at one point, I developed a working relationship with the retired wife of a local doctor. She had learned about the appointments and quickly became a regular.

Week after week, she would bring in her laptop or a mobile device with a list of questions and things she wanted to learn. I helped her with everything from organizing her photo albums to adding friends on Facebook. At one point, she decided her MacBook was getting too slow, and it was time to replace it.

"What kind of computer do you use?" she asked me during an appointment.

"I have a Dell laptop," I said.

"Does it work well? Do you like it?"

"Yeah, I like it. It works well for what I use it for. Email, the Internet, word processing."

"Would you recommend it?"

"Well," I said, "It has a Windows operating system. It's quite different than a MacBook."

"But if you use it and like it, it must be good. I think I'll get a Dell."

Now, I typically don't make a habit of recommending specific products to patrons, but I found it a little flattering that she trusted my opinion. Even though I warned her there's typically a steep learning curve for those who've switched from one operating system to another, she walked into my office the next week with a brand-new Dell laptop. She hadn't even taken it out of the box yet.

"I thought you could help me set it up," she announced after sitting in one of my office chairs with the box on her lap.

"All right, let's see what you've gotten yourself into."

She placed the box on my desk and nudged it toward me.

"Oh no," I said, nudging it back her way. "This is your computer. I'll talk you through it."

We spent the better part of an afternoon running the computer's setup process, covering the basics, and transferring photos. She had a lot of questions but seemed to be getting the hang of it. She left my office hesitant but satisfied with what she learned.

Two weeks later, she walked into my office with a new MacBook.

"I just couldn't get used to it," she admitted.

Kindles and Nooks and iPads, Oh My!

Kindles, Nooks, iPads, and digital content just started to gain popularity during my first few years at the Lawrence Library. While leaders in the library field were busy projecting the impact on library print collections, I was on the front lines helping patrons navigate the world of e-books and downloadable audiobooks and the plethora of devices on which to access them.

Back then, the library belonged to a consortium led by the State Library of Kansas, which contracted with OverDrive, Inc. to provide access to digital content to patrons of participating libraries. Then the State Library's relationship with OverDrive fell through, and they began negotiating with other platforms. They eventually announced 3M Cloud Library, which only had e-books, and OneClickdigital, the audiobook platform from Recorded Books, as the new providers.

So, after getting used to one platform and its instructions, we—and our patrons—had to learn completely different processes for getting content onto devices from not one, but two new platforms. I became one of the go-to librarians for all things digital among the reference staff after beta testing the products.

If patrons had their devices in hand at the library, that was easy. Even though the downloading process varied and I was never completely sure which file formats were compatible with which devices, I usually was able to help a patron to his or her satisfaction.

Trying to help people over the phone was a whole different experience.

I remember spending a significant portion of one evening's desk shift walking a caller through downloading an audiobook from the new OneClickdigital platform to his iPod—a task that wasn't quite as easy as the service's name made it sound. First, we had to determine whether he had an active account.

"I just got used to OverDrive, and you've changed it up on me," he said. "I'm not as quick as I used to be on these things. I thought I signed up for this OneClick thing and downloaded a book, but now I think I deactivated it. I can't find it anywhere. Could I have deleted my account on accident?"

"No, I don't think so," I said. "Your account is your library card number and PIN. Are you on the OneClick website? Can you try logging in for me?"

"Yes, I think I can do that."

I listened as he clicked, typed, and talked himself through signing into the website.

"Okay, I'm in!"

"Great!" I said. "Do you see a button that says, 'My shelf'? If you checked out a book, it should be there."

"Oh yes, there it is. Now how do I get it on my iPod?"

"Did you install the media manager on your computer?" I asked.

He admitted he didn't know what that was, so I then had to explain how to download and sign in through the desktop application. Once he accomplished that, we had to change the default settings so he could transfer the audiobooks.

"Find the settings," I said, "and look for account preferences. You need to check the box next to 'Set

OneClickdigital media manager as the default audio player.'"

After he got that taken care of, I directed him to his list of checked out items where he could click a button that would initiate the download.

"Now you need to find the .zip folder," I explained.

"The what?"

"It's a compressed folder. Do you know how to unzip those?"

Nope. I talked him through that and then also adding the folder to his iTunes library. At that point, he was finally able to transfer the audiobook to his device.

"Oh man," he said. "This is way too complicated."

"Yeah, but think you have the hang of it now?"

"To be honest, no," he sighed. "But I appreciate the help."

"I'm glad we could figure this out for you. Feel free to call again if you need further assistance!"

I never heard from him again, but after all that, I can't say I'd blame him for not giving it another go.

Chapter 9
Collection Services

Spoiler alert: this is probably *the* most exciting chapter of this book. Why? Because it's all about books and other library materials! Oh, and those who are responsible for acquiring them and making them accessible to you.

On a very basic level, Collection Services oversees the birth and death of items in a library. Exciting! Collection development librarians select and review items, acquisitions librarians or assistants place orders and track funds, and catalogers load bibliographic records into the database and prepare items for the shelves.

When items are in poor shape or are no longer fit for the collection, they make their way back to Collection Services for repair, replacement, or deaccessioning. Sad face. But that's the circle of library life.

Tucked away on the lower level, the Collection Services offices at the pre-renovated Lawrence Library didn't appeal to me when I first started. I wanted to help people directly, and processing items, proofreading catalog records, and analyzing data in a cubicle in a room with few windows and fluorescent lighting was too far from that action.

I couldn't imagine myself spending hours of my life in what I thought of as the dark catacombs of the library. But life changed, opportunities arose, I found my way back to LPL, and now I'm head of Cataloging and Collection Development, a subset of Collection Services.

I've grown to love working behind the scenes and helping make decisions about the core of the library's service: the collection. I get to lead a team of skilled selectors and radical catalogers who are passionate about providing a diverse and accessible collection and adapting to the changing needs of the community. And we have windows!

Because we don't work with the public as much, it's safe to say our jobs are a little calmer. When everyone's focused on their ordering, cataloging, and processing, the department falls into a quiet peace that's only occasionally interrupted by the beep of a barcode scanner or the zip-hum of a label printer.

That's not to say, though, that we don't see our fair share of excitement.

Don't Fear the Change, Embrace It

Most of that excitement comes in the form of change. Whether it's rearranging furniture, using a new call number format, altering a procedure, or updating computers, nothing can throw the department into a tizzy like change.

Before I started in my new role as head of the department, the library's leadership team had begun the process of migrating to a new integrated library system (the database that manages all bibliographic, item, and patron records). The ILS being the center of all our collection-related procedures, migrating to a new one is one of the biggest changes you could implement. My staff was not excited.

Having relied on the current ILS for the past ten years, learning its intricacies, adapting to its limitations, and using it for almost every function of their jobs, the catalogers and the acquisitions assistant would be affected the most. They weren't looking forward to learning a whole new system. However, it was out of our hands. The software provider planned to discontinue the ILS to focus on a new product, and the library's admin team had no choice but to explore other options.

Thankfully (and only thankfully because I had absolutely no experience migrating to a new ILS), much of the legwork was completed before I took over. A cross-departmental task force reviewed options, selected a new vendor, and began the process of preparing the data for migration. By the time I settled into my position, we were ready to complete weeks of web-based training and prepare for the vendor's technicians to implement the ILS.

Administration, acquisitions, cataloging, circulation, reports. We spent three to six hours a day watching training tutorials for each module or process and after each, walked away from the room unsure of how much we had retained. We didn't have access to a test version of the ILS until closer to the migration date. Without the hands-on practice, we were lost.

While jumping into an ILS migration not two months into a new position was certainly intimidating, it ended up being a benefit for me. Not having had as much experience working on the back end of the previous system, I felt like I was playing catchup with my staff. Once we transitioned to the new one, we were all on the same page learning together.

The actual migration went smoothly. The technicians took three days to pull the data, manipulate it to fit the new ILS, and get everything back up and running. We couldn't check out to patrons during that time, but the admin team didn't want to completely close access to the building, especially since we were migrating in the hottest part of summer. They turned the auditorium into a small library with a browsing collection of magazines and newspapers, Internet computers, and donated books from the Friends organization.

Once the system was up and running, getting the hang of it was another story. Some modules and processes were more straightforward than others. Circulation was ready to go the first day, cataloging took a couple of weeks, but acquisitions hung us up for almost a month. Requiring a complicated series of reports and procedures, the ordering process, when done properly, pulls records from vendor websites, downloads them into the database, and makes them visible in the catalog for patrons to place holds. Central to the department's functions, we couldn't move forward without it.

Our acquisitions assistant, my manager, and I spent days poring through the manual, watching training videos, and asking for help on listservs. When, through trial and error, we finally got it functioning properly, the whole department celebrated.

To this day, the acquisitions assistant jokingly says we should migrate back to the old ILS when he runs into an issue. Thankfully, that's not an option.

What's in a Label?

In Collection Services, even the smallest changes can lead to the most involved decision-making processes. Take, for example, labels. From award decals to genre stickers, labels help patrons browse collections and find certain items in the stacks. Within my first few months in cataloging and collection development, I learned just how complicated they can be.

As a standing practice, catalogers put "new" stickers on all recently added items. After six months or so, frontline staff would pull those items from the new shelves and remove the stickers. Catalogers used different variations of stickers over the years, based on availability, color preference, adhesiveness, and other criteria.

By the time I started as the department coordinator, catalogers were ready to give up on them altogether. The back and forth was too frustrating. One product simply didn't stick. The edges curled up and eventually, they fell off. Then items marked "new" in the catalog found their way to the regular shelves and caused frustration for those trying to find them.

Another product proved to be exactly the opposite. These were so sticky you had to drown them in adhesive remover to get them off. Staff who removed items from the new shelves argued that it was too time-consuming, plus we were spending more and more money on adhesive remover pens everyone preferred.

With these frustrations in mind, our lead cataloger was determined to put an end to them. However, that decision was easier said than done.

The first issue: tracking when items were acquired. Catalogers' current process involved writing the number of the month the item was added to the collection. This helped frontline staff when pulling items from the new shelves to update.

The solution: our lead cataloger suggested that they print the month and year permanently on the spine label, underneath the call number.

Then we had to think about the materials sorter. This massive machine checks in and conveys books to a series of bins in which items are dropped according to their collections. Our materials handling staff then empty the bins onto carts which are delivered to front-line departments. With the current setup, new adult books were dropped in a separate bin, but new children's and young adult books were sorted into the same bins as the older books in those collections. The new sticker was a clear indication that the items belong on the new shelf.

The solution was simple though. After discontinuing the use of new stickers, all new books would be sorted into the same bin, regardless of audience age. It would mean a small increase in foot traffic for the Materials Handling team, but they were okay with it.

So, were we ready to end the stickers then? Nope.

Our new fiction collections check out for two weeks while everything else checks out for four. The new stickers on the fiction indicated the shorter loan periods. The readers' services team, which manages the fiction collection, reasoned that the lack of stickers would frustrate patrons who rely on them to know what's due sooner and to prioritize their reading.

This is where we had to ask the front-line staff to compromise. We suggested adding signage to the new shelves explaining the shorter checkout periods and encouraging patrons to print their receipts or check their accounts online. If staff received a lot of negative feedback, I assured them, then we'd go back to the drawing board.

So, we did it. We ended the "new" stickers!

This entire decision-making process took about three months. Before starting in Cataloging and

Collection Development, I had no idea that a choice as small as a sticker could be so complex. I'm happy to report that, to the delight of staff who don't have to peel them off each month, we received little to no feedback and we've been "new" sticker-free for two years.

What the #$@% Did They Do to This Book?

The most exciting part of working in Cataloging and Collection Development is seeing the crazy things that happen to ~~out~~ the library's materials.

A vast majority of the items in a library's collection live long happy lives on the shelves and circulate dozens if not hundreds of times before making their way down to Collection Services to be considered for withdrawal. Unfortunately, a number do see an untimely demise at the hands of our patrons.

On any given day, we see books with torn pages, stains, and broken spines, as well as media with scratches, cracked hubs, and broken cases. Less regularly, but not uncommon, are the items that have been mercilessly chewed by an animal or small child, dropped in a bathtub or swimming pool, or otherwise drastically damaged.

If I would give her permission, my cataloging assistant who sorts through them wouldn't hesitate to roll the carts of damaged items out into the street and set them on fire. Burning books is a big no-no, but if it's drenched in a mysterious, possibly pathogenic substance? We'll seriously reconsider.

Whether horrifying or hilarious, here are a few memorable cases that have come across our desks:

1. Melted mylar and burnt cover, the result of a book being placed on the burner of a stove

2. Random nouns scribbled out with a pen and replaced with anatomical terms in a book on basketball

3. A DVD case missing its artwork with a note reading, "Patron's child 'ate the artwork'"

4. A book with half of its pages dog-eared

5. A large stain sealed to a picture book cover with clear packaging tape

6. The cozy mystery *The Cracked Spine* by Paige Shelton with…a cracked spine

7. A young adult novel called *Quarantine* by Lex Thomas quarantined in a Ziplock bag because of a jelly-like substance on the fore-edge

8. The annotation "is one of the stupidest books ever printed" scribbled on the title page of a novel

9. Two items in a Ziplock bag with the note, "Both have holds—smells like dead fish"
10. Another Ziplock bag with the note, "Bloodstains"
11. A fantasy novel with a coded message scrawled on the inside of the front cover and end pages

While we don't condone writing in library books, that coded message provided weeks of entertainment for our department. Staff who enjoy trivia and challenges took turns attempting to crack the code. One of the cataloging assistants shared it on Twitter, it made its way to Reddit, and then it was picked up by a German science blogger! The blogger transcribed it, performed a frequency analysis, and put it through a few decryption tools, all of which rendered no sensible result. The hidden message has remained a mystery to this day.

Part III:
Library Director Tales

Chapter 10

[In Ralph Wiggum's Voice]: "I'm a Director!"

"And this is your office," the city manager says.

We're on the second floor of the expanded Carnegie building standing next to a wood-trimmed door near the reference desk. I glance around at the cozy chairs, ornate columns, display cabinets, and the stacks in the distance. The quarter-after chime of a grandfather clock rings throughout the otherwise silent library.

He hands me the key after unlocking the door, and my breath catches.

Now, this is an office! I think to myself.

It's huge. Original cabinets and shelves line the walls from floor to ceiling, and a large floating light fixture hovers above a gigantic oak desk. A framed stained-glass image of the city square and bandstand hangs in the window between the reading room and my office.

My office.

"The last director was here all the time," the city manager says. "You really don't have to be here all the time."

Oh, but I could live here!

Walking into the Oskaloosa Public Library on my first day as director, I had to gather my confidence like a cardigan around my shoulders. Soft-spoken and timid as I was, I didn't want to let on that I knew very little of what was expected of me.

I couldn't believe how lucky I was to work in such a beautiful library. First built in 1903, the Carnegie building was renovated and expanded in 1997 to twice its size. The architects for the project designed the expansion with brick, masonry, and woodwork that matched the original structure. High ceilings, dropped lighting, ornate wood columns, and, as I've already mentioned, a director's office to die for!

A large circulation counter, an expansive children's collection, a play area, a storytime room, and staff workspaces were on the ground level. The adult and teen collections, a reading room, and a local history room were on the second floor, and there were meeting rooms on the third. My favorite spot, other than my office, was a reading area in the back with tall windows that overlooked a magnolia tree in the neighboring yard.

While touring the building that first day, the elegance and history of the building only reminded me of my inexperience. I had never supervised staff, I had never managed a budget, and forget building maintenance. Somehow, though, I convinced the board of trustees that a twenty-seven-year-old with only three years of library work behind him was right for the job.

Now I had to prove it to myself.

After handing over the key to the office, briefly introducing me to the staff in the building, and quickly briefing me on current issues, the city manager left me to my own devices. I sat behind my new desk and thought to myself, *Well, what do I do now?* Up until that point, I had only ever worked under the direction of a supervisor. I had never structured my day.

I guess I could fill out the rest of this paperwork. I thought. *Or I could ask someone to show me around the rest of the building.*

Then I remembered my interview with the board of trustees. One of them asked me what I would accomplish first as the director. Instead of new programs, policy updates, or sweeping changes, I told them my first goal would be to learn as much as possible about the staff, the library, and the community. How could I gain the trust of the organization if I didn't take the time to get to know the ones who I'd be leading in this position?

With that in mind, I began by scheduling one-on-one meetings with staff. From the part-time pages to the long-time children's librarian, I wanted to meet each of them individually to learn what they did for the library. I could have simply read job descriptions, but I wanted to make sure they got to know me as well. I wanted to be approachable.

The administrative assistant described her role as if it were taken straight from the pages of children's fantasy novel. Having worked for several years as a teacher at a Catholic high school, she returned to Oskaloosa to move into her childhood home with her sister and take care of her aging parents. She earned a full-time position at the library after volunteering, then working part-time, and then taking over when the previous administrative assistant retired.

I met with her first so we could review recent board minutes and so she could teach me her system for invoicing and tracking finances for the library's budget. Her office was adjacent to mine and barely had enough space for the filing cabinets and desk that filled it. I took a seat next to her as she arranged thick notebooks and folders on her desktop.

"These are my cats," she announced, pointing to five framed five-by-sevens propped on the wood of her office windowsill. "Or I should say, the five cats who let my sister and I share a home with them."

I knew then we were going to get along famously.

"I'll have to introduce you to my Echo," I said.

"Ooh, you have a cat?" She smiled.

"Yes! I've had her since I was in high school. She'll be fourteen in April."

"I'd love to meet her!"

She then named each of hers, pointing them out in the photos on the windowsill. We could have bonded over cats all morning, but after she briefly described their personalities, we returned to the business at hand.

"I like to call myself the keeper of the keys and the winder of the clock," she said while opening a desk drawer. An assortment of keys dangling from numbered hooks lined the inside of the drawer.

"I love that," I said.

"As you can see, I keep track of all the keys to the building." She plucks an ornate silver one from one of the hooks. "And on Tuesdays and Thursdays, I use this to wind the grandfather clock in the lobby."

Her job, I learned, encompassed much more than that. Because of her teaching background, one of the previous directors assigned her maintenance of the small teen collection in addition to tracking the library's finances. She also served as secretary to the board of trustees, and, like most staff, assisted patrons at both the reference and circulation desks.

She used both the financial software on her computer and handwritten ledgers to track the library's revenue and expenditures. Hence, the assortment of notebooks and folders she had laid out on her desk.

"There are two types of accountants I've been told," she said to me. "There are those who, when they found a missing penny, would let it go. Then there are those who would spend all night searching for that penny."

"Sounds like a lot of work for a penny."

"That's me. I'm very careful with the figures," she said. "Otherwise, I'll have the city clerk after me."

She opened one of the ledgers. Columns of line item descriptions written in careful cursive lined the page next to neatly written numbers.

"The library has two major funding sources," she explained and pointed to one of the ledgers. "The general fund, which comes from the city, and the memorial fund, which is all other income, including donations, replacement fees, and money from the book sale. Each fund is broken into different line items and assigned fund codes..."

I admit I didn't commit everything to memory that first meeting, but over time I got the hang of the system with her help. Because her office was next to mine, and because we bonded over our mutual love of cats, we developed a close working relationship during my time at Oskaloosa. From the beginning, she was a constant source of encouragement and confidence, for which I was immensely grateful.

The other staff included a children's librarian, a library technician, a building maintenance manager, three full-time library assistants, three part-time assistants, and two pages. I spent the first couple of weeks meeting with them and learning procedures by shadowing them at the desks. It was at that point that I learned that I wasn't there to tell them what to do.

Aside from the part-time assistants, everyone had more library experience than I did. Three of the full-time staff had been working at the library longer than I'd been alive! Fully coming to realize this made me think hard about my approach to leading the organization. They knew what they were doing, and they didn't need some twenty-seven-year-old, freshly degreed kid bossing them around. I had to figure out quickly the difference between being a manager and being a leader.

When it came time for my first all-staff meeting, my confidence remained low, and my nerves ran high. Even though I had met everyone, and they seemed to receive me well, I still wasn't used to the idea of managing twelve other people. As everyone gathered around the table, I grew more and more nervous. But I took a deep breath and began the meeting.

"Good morning everyone," I began. "I just have a few things on my agenda…"

I kept to the meeting format that the administrative assistant explained the staff preferred. After I finished with my agenda, each staff member had the opportunity to bring up questions or topics for discussion. I don't remember exactly what we covered in that first meeting, but the administrative assistant stopped me afterward.

"That was the most productive meeting we've had in a long time," she said. She smiled and patted my shoulder. "I'm so glad you're here."

She couldn't have known how much that boosted my confidence.

Chapter 11

The Buck Stops Where?

Day three, or somewhere around there, and I'm sitting in my office reviewing board reports when the cataloging assistant knocks on my door. "Hey William," she says, "a patron returned this DVD, but the labels have been peeled off."

She sets the case on my desk. Other than the missing barcode label, the case and DVD are in good condition.

"Do we usually bill for this?" I ask.

"We have in the past," she says, "but it's up to you. You're the boss."

Those three words echo in my head.

You're the boss. You're the boss. You're the boss, William.

This isn't me being conceited. This is me realizing that "being the boss" means making decisions, and for someone for which that has never come easy, this is me realizing, for the first time, the depth of what I've gotten myself into.

Yes, it's a simple decision. Bill the patron for the peeled labels, or don't. Hold the patron responsible and possibly upset them, or let it go and possibly frustrate staff by not keeping consistent with past policy. What to do?

I know what you're thinking. *If this guy had this much trouble with this decision, how the heck did he run a library?*

By learning one big decision at a time, I'd say. It might seem counterintuitive, but once I knew I could handle things like hiring staff, overseeing building projects, putting together a budget proposal, and leading a community-wide strategic planning process, the smaller, day-to-day decisions like this one became much easier.

And, thankfully, I wasn't on my own.

Big Decision #1: Hiring

What first-time manager doesn't struggle with their first hiring decisions? Heck, even some managers I know who've been doing it for years still find it challenging. I had the fortune of getting to hire right off the bat as a new director.

Before I started, one of the part-time pages had left their position to attend college, which meant the library had an opening to fill. I admit I didn't expect to be on the other side of the hiring process so soon, and I didn't know where to begin.

Luckily, the library technician who oversaw circulation and trained new pages had saved a position description, job ad, skills test, and interview questions from previous openings. I only had to update and submit the ad to the city's HR clerk, who posted the listing, accepted applications, and handled most onboarding.

The fun part, for me, began with reviewing the applications.

"Okay, so how do you want to do this?" I asked the library technician after I had retrieved the stack from City Hall.

"Well, the decision is up to you," she said.

"But you'll be training and overseeing the new page," I said. "Aren't you typically involved with the hiring process?"

"Yes," she said, "but the last directors reviewed the applications."

"Well, let me take a look at these," I said, "and pick my top candidates. Then I'll let you review them, and we'll see what we come up with?"

"Sounds good to me." I could tell she was glad to be more involved in the hiring process, and I was glad to have an experienced hand to help me make the decision.

A long-held hiring practice, a ten-question quiz that tested numerical and alphabetical organization skills, helped us narrow down candidates who, as far as we could tell on paper, were all suitable for an interview. (At the time, I didn't think about how this practice was an unfair barrier to those with learning disabilities or those who experience test anxiety. While I'm sure we would have made accommodations, I realize now it should have been a goal to rethink it.)

The interview questions were a combination of practical and cringeworthy. Why are you interested in working at the library? Can you tell us about a time when you were responsible? Do you foresee this position as long-term or short-term? A woman comes up to you, shows you a rash on her arm, and asks for advice. What do you do? What would you do if you noticed two teens cuddling in a chair and kissing?

Even after listening to our four final candidates awkwardly answer these questions, the decision proved difficult. I knew that each of them, given the chance, would have done a fantastic job. But we only had one available position, and so the library assistant and I picked over their responses and offered the position to the one in which we mutually had the most confidence.

And so, I had my first experience hiring staff. It did little to prepare me, though, for the next staff opening: a replacement for a popular, long-time children's librarian.

An Intro to Project Management

I also stepped into the middle of a contentious landscaping project when I arrived at Oskaloosa. A generous community member had bought and donated property adjacent to the library's parking lot, and the Friends of the Library raised funds for benches, a gazebo, and landscaping for a reading garden by selling inscribed bricks.

Contention arose when the previous director unilaterally approved plans for a pavilion instead of a gazebo. It looked more like a bus stop, and some weren't happy with it. The director's intent, though, was an outdoor performance space for children's programming. Unfinished designs included stone auditorium-style seating, picnic tables, and greenery that would bring the space together.

So, there I was, now in charge of overseeing the completion of a reading garden with a pavilion that no one liked. Where was I to start? Should I have the pavilion removed, wasting the thousands of dollars that were spent on it? Should I move forward with the designs as intended? What could be done to ensure the Friends board members and other stakeholders were satisfied with the project when completed?

The answer: a committee.

Having served as interim director in the months before I started, the city manager had already formed a committee to oversee the completion of the garden. With representation from staff, the library board of trustees, the Friends of the Library board, and, since the land was technically the property of the city, the city council, the committee collectively made decisions on how to move forward with the project.

It was now my responsibility to lead that committee. Everyone agreed that moving forward with the plans as they were was the best course of action. By the following spring, the landscaper completed the brick and stonework and planted trees and shrubs, and we invited the community for a grand opening. But that wasn't the end of it.

As the inscribed bricks expanded in the heat of summer, they began to crack. Our single building maintenance manager had trouble keeping up with the pruning, raking, and upkeep of the garden. Friends board members and staff expressed concerns about the openness of the space and recommended enclosing it with an iron fence. When we installed that fence, a neighbor drove their car into it. Things kept going wrong.

Despite all of that, the reading garden did serve as a nice space for programs and events in the warmer months. We packed it with kids and activities for our summer reading kick-off parties, held storytimes and presentations in the pavilion, scouts groups planted flowers in the spring, and the local Key Club volunteered to help clean up the area regularly. A couple even asked to use the space for their wedding!

Though the project may have started contentiously, through transparency and involving others in the planning, I was glad to see the committee, the library staff, and the community feel ownership of it and grow to be proud of the reading garden.

Budgeting 101

As the end of the year approached, the city manager informed me that I needed to start preparing the next year's budget. The city's fiscal year started in July, but the budget planning and approval process would need to be completed in the spring.

By that point, I'd only been on the job for a couple of months. Spending and tracking the library's money was the easy part. Planning and justifying a year's worth of expenditures, I would come to discover, wasn't so simple. The library's budget would need to be drafted, reviewed by the city manager and clerk, approved by the library board, and then approved by the city council as a part of the city's budget.

Again, I wasn't alone, but from my inexperienced perspective, it was a monumental and important process that made me nervous. With help from the administrative assistant, I started by reviewing the current year's budget and comparing it to the expenditures of previous years. After adjusting a few line items, I met with the budget and finance committee of the board of trustees for their feedback. They, and then the city manager and clerk, surprisingly had very little concern with my figures.

The real fun began with a half-day budget retreat with the city council. And by fun, I mean hours of sitting and listening to council members discuss funding for every department except for mine. Since the library was a department of the city, I had to be present in case there were any questions about the library's proposed budget, but that rarely was the case. Even though our projected expenditures were the third-largest behind the fire and police departments, the library's budget paled in comparison to the other departments'.

In the end, the library board and the city council approved the budget with few questions and no concerns. I couldn't believe how straightforward it turned out to be.

Planning Strategically

After the reading garden and the budget, my next big project was leading a strategic planning process. To receive state accreditation and funding, the library needed to have a completed or updated plan every three years. It was specifically mentioned in the job ad for my position, and so, after taking a few months to acclimate to the library, plus smooth out a few bumps (e.g. hire new staff), it was time to get it done.

This is where I can confidently say I used what I learned in library school (imagine that!). Not knowing where else to start, I borrowed the whole process from the Organization Theories for Administering Information Agencies group project. With the board's approval, I formed a committee and laid out an incredibly detailed sixth-month agenda based on the one my classmates and I had put together for our fictional library.

Like with the reading garden committee, I wanted to make sure all stakeholders were involved in the process, so the strategic planning committee included representation from staff, the library board, the Friends of the Library, and the city council. With their input, I divided them into task forces for environmental scanning, developing and distributing a survey, coordinating focus groups, inventorying the collection, and writing the final goals and objectives.

Over the next five months, we visited neighboring city libraries and potential partners in the community, distributed the survey online and at the service desks, reviewed the library's collections, and invited different cross-sections of the community to participate in discussions led by a representative from the state library. In the end, we had pages and pages of comments, suggestions, collection analyses, and data about the use of the library and participants' needs and aspirations for the community.

The writing task force then took the last month to pore through all the comments and data, develop five broad goals, and write up specific objectives to complete each of the goals. We compiled all the data, the goals, and the objectives into one massive three-year strategic plan document, and I proudly presented it to the board for approval.

It was done!

In hindsight, the complex process and massive document may have been a bit over the top for what was needed for a small-town library. Previous plans, I discovered, were much simpler, listing broad goals without much detail. But I wanted something much more specific, and, I admit, I wanted to prove to the board, the city council, and the staff that the library was in good hands. That I had a plan.

Chapter 12
The Many Hats of a Small Library Director

I often describe the job at Oskaloosa as the Goldilocks of library director positions. The organization wasn't so large that my time was completely occupied with meetings and administrative tasks, and it wasn't so small that I wasn't able to do what I wanted because of a lack of resources. It was perfect for gaining a well-rounded experience.

From shelving materials to working the circulation desk to ordering books for the collection to teaching computer classes to developing policy with the board to advocating for funding at city council meetings, I wanted to do it all. I probably could have delegated more, but I wanted to be completely invested and involved in the operations of the library.

There were times when I even surprised staff who were used to previous directors spending most of their time in the office. The first day I started to shelve a cart of books when one of the pages was out sick, the library technician was shocked.

"What are you doing?" she asked.

"I'll take care of this cart," I responded. "Is that okay?"

"Yes. It's just…I haven't seen a director shelve books in a long time."

"Really?"

"If you have other things to do, we'll be okay."

"No, I'm good," I said. "I like shelving books. It'll help me get to know the collection."

And I promise that was an honest answer. Now that I was an actual director of a small library, like Forney Hull in *Where the Heart Is*, I wanted to get to know the collection as quickly as possible so I could help patrons as he did. What better way than by returning items to their proper locations on the shelves?

And just like Forney, I had no issue getting my slacks dirty. Seriously, if you've ever crawled along the floor to scan Dewey call numbers for a book's proper location, you'll know what I'm talking about.

Building a Community's Collection

Aside from managing staff and working with the board of trustees, developing the collection was another major responsibility I held as director. And like those other responsibilities, it was intimidating for this newbie at first. The only library I had experience buying books for was my own, so I had to learn quickly how to go beyond my preferences and tastes when selecting materials.

Oh, and I also had a significantly higher budget. But that was the easy part, I remember telling myself. Simply divide the amount that's left in the budget by the number of weeks left in the year, and that's how much you get to spend each order day.

The truth? It wasn't *that* easy.

There's a lot to consider when developing a collection. Are you keeping up with titles that are in demand? What areas of the collection need improvement? What sections circulate well and what sections could be cut back? Are you buying the kinds of books that the community likes or are they going to gather dust on the shelves?

Fortunately, there were several ways to gather input to inform decisions. Circulation reports from the library's database told me what collections circulated well, and I used expenditure reports to keep track of where I was spending funds. We also accepted suggestions for the collection, which helped me learn specific interests.

Using a form on the website or printed ones at the desks, patrons could tell me specific titles they wished to see in the collection. Because some were more prolific in their suggestions than others, I developed a systematic way of approving and ordering what people wanted. Over time, I got to know more about what the community liked.

Some patrons also came to me directly to talk to me about the collection. Not too long after I started, I got a visit from a concerned woman who, at first, made me question my collection development practices. The library assistant who was working at the reference desk led her to my office and asked if I had a moment to speak with her.

After I invited her into my office, and she introduced herself, she said, "I wanted to speak with you about the collection."

Uh oh, I thought to myself. *What did I do wrong?*

"I come to the library often, and I appreciate having so many resources available," she started. "But I'm concerned about the religion section."

"Were you not able to find what you were looking for?" I asked.

"No, not exactly," she said. "There are a lot of different books there, but this is a predominantly

Christian community, and I believe the religion section should reflect that."

I was a bit taken aback and didn't know what to say. She proceeded to name a few Christian theologians and writers, explaining that the collection lacked notable Christian resources. I nodded, trying to make sure she knew I was listening to her.

"Thank you for your suggestions," I said when she finished. "I did just start ordering here, but it is my goal to make sure the collection reflects the needs and interests of the community. If you know of any specific titles, I'd be happy to consider them for the collection."

"I don't have any off the top of my head," she said. "I just think a better job could be done."

"Okay," I said. "If you do think of any, we've got forms at the reference desk."

I knew my response wasn't the one she wanted by the way she left my office. While she had a point about the collection needing to reflect the community, I got the hint that she would prefer there were no other religions represented on the shelves. That's honestly when I decided not to take too much stock in her criticism, and I never did receive any specific suggestions from her.

Thankfully, not all patron feedback was negative. Any time a patron got back to me about a suggestion I had purchased, they were grateful and sometimes even overjoyed. That was the best part of ordering for the collection, knowing you made someone's day by providing them access to a book, DVD, CD, or resource they may not be able to obtain through other means.

Getting with the Program

Planning and hosting programs also proved to be a steep learning curve for this newbie director. Having moved 265 miles to the town to take the position, I knew little about the interests of the community and had no idea what events would draw people to the library. I didn't know where to start and made no effort until a local author contacted me.

A martial arts instructor who wrote crime novels on the side called and asked to do a book signing and tae kwon do demonstration to promote his recently self-published release.

"People love watching martial arts," he exclaimed over the phone. "And my book is about a private detective with a black belt who investigates the murder of her boyfriend. It's sure to draw people in!"

Figuring I had an easy program in my hands, I printed up fliers, shared the event on the library's Facebook page, and talked it up at the desk. On the afternoon of the event, I set up twenty-five chairs, optimistically thinking we could set out more if needed. I greeted the author and helped him arrange a display of the books he brought to sell. Then we waited.

No more than five people showed up.

Through the whole presentation, I kept thinking, *What did I do wrong here? Was it the timing? Did I not share it enough on Facebook? Should I have printed more fliers?* I was sorry so few people were there and felt even worse that no one bought any of his books.

The author didn't seem to mind, though. He enthusiastically talked about his novel and demonstrated tae kwon do moves with a teenager in the audience.

After the program, I lamented the results with my staff. They reminded me that the value of a program isn't always in the number of seats filled and that I shouldn't let low turnout stop me from planning more programs. I've learned since that program attendance is guesswork at the best. Even if you require registration beforehand, you never know exactly how many people are going to show up.

I eventually learned more about the community and grew to love planning events. My favorite program was a partnership with a local beer pub. They had been wanting to bring a tasting of local beers to the library, and I had the brilliant idea of pairing it with the perfect presentation. I learned, through a state listserv for librarians, about an engaging speaker and author who had released a new book on prohibition in eastern Iowa.

With Oskaloosa leaning more on the conservative side, though, I had to do a bit of research to make sure the program would be both legal and received well before getting it on the calendar. I wanted to get creative with programming at the library, but I also didn't want the library board getting complaints about the director turning the library into a speakeasy.

First, I spoke with the state's bureau of alcoholic beverages who said that if the samples were under an ounce and served only to patrons 21 years or older, the event wouldn't violate any state ordinances. Next, I checked with the city attorney and the public works director to see if anything in the zoning ordinances or the city code prohibited the sampling. Then I verified that the event would be covered under general liability in the city's insurance policy.

Finally, I checked in with the city manager. By that point, he knew what I was planning and had already spoken to a couple of city council members, and they liked that I was doing new and different things to bring people into the library. It was a go!

On the night of the event, I feared it would be another tae kwon do crime novel turnout. As I arranged the chairs and watched the pub staff set up their kegs in the kitchenette, the clock ticked closer and closer to the start time and just a handful of people trickled into the meeting room. Then a few more. And a few more. And then even more.

Before I knew it, all the seats were full, and the room buzzed with excitement for the presentation and the tasting. Everything went off without a hitch. Attendees enjoyed the program, and I didn't receive a single complaint. It was a good feeling knowing I had brought people in the community together to learn and connect.

Somebody's Gotta Do It

Of all the responsibilities I covered during my time, I admit janitorial ones were my least favorite. When our sole building manager was out sick, I found myself refilling paper towels, vacuuming and mopping floors, and dusting shelves. Nothing to complain about, I know.

One December afternoon, though, before I was about to take off for the holidays, the cataloging assistant, who was covering the reference desk, knocked on my office door.

"Uh, William, I hate to tell you this," she said. "But a patron just told me he made a mess in the men's room."

"Oh lord. What kind of mess?"

"He said he got sick."

Why was she telling me? Because the building manager, who wouldn't have blinked an eye at a mess in the bathroom, had already left.

"Oh jeez," I said, "I don't even like cleaning up after my cats."

As much as I dreaded it, though, I wasn't about to ask one of the library assistants to take care of it. I gathered the mop, bucket, gloves, and a mask and did my best to clean up the mess. Then, knowing we'd be closing in less than an hour, I hung an "Out of Order" sign on the stall. Not one hundred percent confident in my ability to effectively sanitize the space, I didn't want to risk the chance of getting other patrons sick.

"Thank you for taking care of that," the cataloging assistant said when I emerged from the restroom.

"Never again," I responded.

I had never been more ready for the holidays.

Fortunately, that was probably the most unpleasant mess I had to clean up. And while I'd love to forget it, it did make me appreciate the work that facilities staff do daily to make sure the library is clean and sanitary. Some libraries, especially smaller ones, may not even have facilities staff, so I acknowledge I was lucky there.

Chapter 13

Leaving the Place in One Piece

I have never considered myself a handyman. The extent of my maintenance aptitude is probably changing a light bulb. Unless it's a fluorescent tube in a glass globe hanging ten feet in the air. And especially not if it involves replacing a ballast. Whatever that is.

Fortunately, the library and City Hall employed a full-time building manager that oversaw maintenance and janitorial services at both facilities. He was a Chicago-transplant with a penchant for squirreling away random tools, shelf pieces, bookends, computer parts, and other odds and ends in the library's cramped storage spaces.

Quick to please, the building manager spent much of his time and patience doing the best to make everyone comfortable and happy. This was nearly impossible with the library's temperamental HVAC system, three floors of carpets and restrooms and meeting spaces to clean, and his responsibilities at City Hall.

I let him know from the beginning that I wasn't much of a handyman, but I was willing to learn and help as much as possible when needed. That's how I ended up cleaning a filter in an air handler on the roof within the first month.

Imagine me tiptoeing along the safety beam and climbing back in the third-floor access hatch in my freshly bought slacks and dust-covered oxford shirt, safety goggles on, grease covering my fingertips, ready to cover the reference desk. Quite debonair if you ask me.

That temperamental HVAC system proved to be the bane of my directorship.

When the building was expanded and reno-vated in the late 1990s, the engineers installed what one board member not-so-fondly referred to as a "Library of Congress grade" heating and cooling system. Four boilers, four humidifiers, an air han-dler, and an air conditioner maintained the prime environment for preserving the library's collection no matter the season.

The building manager tried to explain the system to me once. The boilers would run throughout the year, kicking in heat when the air conditioner overcooled the building in the summer. The air handler forced cool, dry air into the building during the mild spring and fall seasons, and the humidifiers prevented static from building in the stacks during the winter.

Don't quote me on that.

Over the next twenty years, though, decisions were made that left the system in less than optimal condition. Differing opinions among local and corporate contractors resulted in a piecemeal and questionable maintenance history. By the time I got there, only two boilers remained and none of the four humidifiers were functioning, previous leadership having opted not to repair or replace them.

The temperature was never consistent throughout the building, and work areas were always either too warm or too cold. During the milder seasons, the air handler caused a piercing whistle as it forced air through the cracks between the wood frames of the original entrance.

We were committed to an expensive preventative maintenance contract with a company I quickly came to mistrust. It seemed like every quarterly visit, their specialists would spend half a day changing out filters and would come away with something that needed to be fixed or specially cleaned or replaced.

When I received an invoice for 150 dollars for updating a phone number, I figured something was up.

"Why are we receiving a bill for updating a contact number?" I remember arguing with their billing office. "This is ridiculous."

"It's industry standard," the person on the other end of the line explained. "That's the hourly rate for our tech specialists."

"One hundred and fifty dollars for entering a number into a computer?"

"It's a bit more complicated than that."

"Surely it didn't take an hour."

"That's the minimum we bill."

"This isn't right," I argued. "I feel like you're taking advantage of us."

Eventually, I spoke with our account manager, and the invoice was waived on the technicality that we weren't reminded of the cost of updating the contact number beforehand. From that point on, I was critical of every suggested repair and invoice.

In reviewing the past five years of the library's relationship with the company, I found that on top of the annual preventative maintenance contract fee, hundreds of thousands of dollars were paid in repairs and replacements.

For a "Library of Congress grade" HVAC, that may have been understandable, but it was clear that the system was no longer up to those standards. I made it my goal to drastically reduce the funds bleeding into their coffers. That proved tough when now and then a boiler quit, or an air handler got struck by lightning.

So yeah, it was news to me that hundred-year-old Carnegie buildings are expensive to maintain. After arranging a boiler replacement, bringing the elevator up to code, calling on an electrician to reroute ground wire to the parking lot light fixtures, and coordinating the repair and painting of the façade of an exterior support column that began to split in half, I began to grow numb to sticker shock.

Thankfully, the director at the time of the building's expansion in the late 1990s worked with the city to invest a million dollars from the local option sales tax that funded the project. The city ordinance allowed for the library to budget a percentage of the interest to "maintain the library facility and its functions and equipment." From air handlers to stone masonry caps, we were covered.

One possible maintenance project, though, had the potential to dip into that principal. On an afternoon within the last few months of my directorship, the building manager knocked on my office door. "Do you have a moment?"

"Hi, yes, please come in."

"Mind if I close the door? I don't want to freak anyone out."

"Yes, that's fine," I said, waving him in. He took a seat across from me.

"William, I think this place is falling apart."

I stared at him.

"I'm not sure it's safe to be open to the public. We might need the fire department to come in and take a look."

"Why's that? What's going on?"

"I've got a reason to believe the addition is coming away from the original building," he explained. "Can I show you?"

He first brought me up to the restrooms on the third floor. "Remember how I thought it was just a bad grout job that needed to be redone in the women's room?"

"Yeah, but we had that fixed, right?"

"Well, I think we have a fault line across the whole level." He pointed to a bump in the carpet near my feet. "Look there."

The bump was about the height of a power cord and spanned the width of the hallway. If he hadn't pointed it out to me, I wouldn't have noticed it.

"There's a similar bump on the other side, near Meeting Room C," he explained. "And the drywall above it is beginning to crack."

The third-floor hallway was a half square with the elevator, restrooms, a kitchenette, meeting spaces and a door to the original stairway off it. We walked around to Meeting Room C, and sure enough, there was the bump in the carpet and a few tiny cracks in the painted drywall. Again, barely noticeable.

"The grout line in the women's room runs right along this line," he said. "It's where the original building meets the concrete of the addition. I'm sure of it."

"And you think it's coming apart?"

"There's more."

From there, he took me to the second floor, where he pointed out another ridge on the carpet. It spanned the entire width of the floor. I couldn't believe I hadn't noticed this one. "I'm guessing this is right below the other one?" I asked.

"Not quite," he responded. "The addition on the third floor is further to the west, where the elevator and Meeting Room C are located. Down here, the fault is along this line."

"You sure it's not just the carpet bunching up?"

"That's what I thought, but there's the fireplace in the genealogy room. Remember how I said the façade is coming unpinned from the wall?"

"It's along this line?"

"Sure is."

At this point, I was beginning to worry that the building manager's suspicions had substance. I didn't believe we were at the point of closing the building, but to calm his nerves, I told him to arrange a walk through with the fire department. I also contacted OPN Architects, the firm that designed the expansion, and asked if they would be willing to visit and review his observations.

What worried me more was the fact that I had started to plan the end of my time in Oskaloosa. My partner had acquired a position back in Lawrence, and I was beginning to look for jobs there too. I knew I couldn't leave, though, if the building needed major work.

When the architects made the trip, they brought along an engineer, and the building manager walked them through the library, pointing out the ridge in the carpets, the cracks in the drywall, and the failing fireplace pinning.

It didn't take long for them to conclude that the building was not falling apart. They understood why the building manager came to suspect that but explained that it was all cosmetic. Twenty-year-old carpets tend to bunch in places. Drywall cracks as buildings shift and settle. Fireplace façades sometimes come unpinned.

Needless to say, I was relieved.

The architects appreciated the opportunity to review the building and left us with a list of improvement projects. The fixes weren't going to be cheap, but they were much more manageable. When I followed through with my resignation in the fall, I was happy to note that, despite my lack of maintenance know-how, the building was still in one piece when I left.

Part IV:
Librarian Rants and Raves

Chapter 14

We Don't Just Sit and Read All Day

I knew I made it big as a librarian when a reporter from Oskaloosa's local news station, run by the city's small private university, came to interview me on my first day as director of the library. Hey, I had never been on the news before!

The following afternoon, though, I cringed as I watched the clip on their YouTube channel. "The new director of the Oskaloosa Public Library started this week," the reporter announced as he walked down an aisle in the stacks toward the camera. "But he doesn't look like your typical librarian."

Cut to a shot of me staring wide-eyed at the reporter off-screen. "I do have a few cardigans in my closet."

I know what you're thinking.

Cardigans? Way to perpetuate the stereotype, William!

The reporter doesn't explain what "your typical librarian" looks like, but I bet he had the bun-wearing, middle-aged, cozily clad and shushing image that's often perpetuated by pop-culture in his head. I won't get into how cringe-worthy the rest of that interview was, mostly on my part, but the clip's probably floating around YouTube, so you can see for yourself.

On the topic of cardigans, though, who doesn't love a nice, comfy sweater that's easy to throw on as a quick solution to fluctuating temperatures? Not *all* librarians, of course, but I have encountered a number who unhesitatingly embrace that stereotype. Try going to an annual gathering of librarians. You'll lose count of the number of cardigans you'll see.

In a quick, informal poll I administered during a keynote I gave for the South Dakota Library Association's 2016 annual conference, for example, sixty percent of the attendees reported they owned at least three cardigans. Thirteen percent reported they owned more than ten, and one elementary school librarian claimed she had more than forty-five! I received similar results when I polled association and library staff audiences in Alabama, Arkansas, Illinois, Missouri, and Oklahoma as well. So, I feel it's safe to say that a love of cardigans isn't necessarily a false or negative librarian stereotype.

Other than the cardigans, we're also commonly known for:

- Glasses
- "Sensible" shoes
- Buns
- Sweater vests
- Bow ties
- Bookish apparel
- Bookish tattoos
- Tote bags
- Cats

All of which, I'd say, is relatively innocuous. Unfortunately, though, the media and the general public tend to cling to several outdated notions about librarians and libraries that are harmful to our image and mission. We're either presented as suppressed, sexual deviants (a.k.a. "sexy librarians"), hipsters, or cardigan-clad, bun-sporting spinsters.

I loathe that we are either old cranky people or cool young hipsters and nothing in between. Rubbish.

— Facebook comment

Even I had to get past the idea, acquired in my youth, that librarians were surly, stern older women who were there just to shush me or tell me where I could or could not sit. It took interacting with library staff regularly to confront and let go of those preconceived notions. The same can be said about libraries. Visiting and using one is the best way to better understand what they are all about.

Nothing gets #LibraryTwitter riled up more than a pundit or politician who claims that no one uses libraries anymore, and they should no longer be funded because the information is now "easily available" online. These claims are often made by people privileged enough to have no need to step foot in a library and probably haven't for years, if ever.

That assertion is also based on the misconception that libraries are only about books and print materials. Those who believe no one uses libraries anymore think of them as repositories of dusty volumes and ancient microfilm reels. While print materials have been at the center of the mission of libraries since the beginning, anyone who visits a modern library regularly knows they go far beyond simply providing access to information this way.

You may have heard the quote from Neil Gaiman, "Google can bring you back 100,000 answers, a librarian can bring you back the right one." I'd add that a librarian also offers you human connection. While computers and algorithms do well to present you with information you "might like," library staff can follow up to make sure your question is answered, your information needs are met, and that you walk away with a book or resource that actually meets your needs. You can build a relationship with a human. Not so much with a machine.

I love when someone who hasn't been to the library in ages remarks on how busy it is. On any given day, you'll see parents reading picture books to their children, teenagers studying or playing games on the computers, older adults learning how to use their mobile devices at the tech help desk, and classes or programs taking place in the meeting spaces. This is all in addition to patrons browsing the stacks of books, magazines, newspapers, DVDs, CDs, and other physical materials available at the library.

I remember a young man applying for a position shelving books. He told me he thought working in a library would be peaceful and was excited about being able to sit in a corner and read. Wha.....?

— Facebook comment

Another common misconception is that library work is stress-free and low-skilled. If you're still convinced that that's the case at this point, please go back a few chapters. You might have missed a few things.

Frankly, though, people who believe that our jobs are stress-free forget that we work with the public. An argument about a fine, a creeper hitting on you at the desk, a complaint about a service or program. While most patrons are pleasant, it takes just one negative interaction to ruin your whole day, and a string of similar incidents can quickly lead to burnout.

Our jobs are also much more complex than people tend to believe. When I first told friends and family that I was going to graduate school for library science, some of them responded, "You have to have a master's degree to be a librarian?" In their minds, librarians shelved books and read all day. If this book hasn't convinced you that's not the case, then I don't know what will.

Sometimes we're lucky if we get the time to read work email. And while there are entry-level positions that don't require an advanced degree and ones specifically for shelving books, most librarian and managerial level positions do require a certain amount of education and experience, depending on the size and location of the library. Whether that's gained through a graduate program or through years of working up through the ranks, most library work isn't something anyone can just walk in off the street and do.

Even the most basic of responsibilities, like shelving, take alphabetization and organizational skills and weeks of training to learn the intricacies of a library's different collections.

Once had a patron speak so quietly, I couldn't hear the question. Finally told her, "You don't have to whisper, no one else here does."

— Facebook comment

People also expect that all libraries should be quiet and that librarians are strict volume enforcers. This image is perpetuated by many commercials set, for whatever reason, in a library. They usually feature a frowning bun-sporting or cardigan-wearing librarian shushing anyone daring to speak above a whisper or scrape a chair across the floor. See also any joke that involves a library or librarian.

Then there's Lori Beth Denberg's hilarious portrayal of "The Loud Librarian" in Nickelodeon's sketch comedy show for kids, *All That.* If you've never seen the sketch, "The Loud Librarian," Ms.

Hushbaum, was a stereotypically clad substitute librarian known for her not so silent tendencies. Under signage that read "Hush," "No talking," or "Shhh," she would engage in noisy activities but ironically yell things like, "Quiet! This is a library!" at kids who made the tiniest sounds.

It's all fun, of course, but it also reinforces the idea that your local librarian will whip out the shushing finger at the slightest noise. While I do admit the prospect of using a megaphone to confront a patron talking loudly on a cell phone is tempting, that's rarely the case.

For better or for worse, the public libraries that I have worked in and many that I've visited aren't completely silent. While most have specific areas that are intended for quiet study and can tend to be quieter during low traffic times, public libraries, at least, have evolved to allow, or even expect, some noise. We want our spaces to be inviting, and accosting people for the slightest noise infractions works against that.

Most librarians don't expect you to ask your questions in hushed tones at the desk and won't glare at you for coughing or sneezing. We'll only whip out that shushing finger as a last resort, I promise.

Chapter 15

What Not to Say to a Librarian and Other Pet Peeves

A patron approaches the circulation desk with a stack of items in her arms. After plopping the stack on the desk, she starts to dig through her purse.

"Are you ready to check out?" I ask.

She continues to dig.

"If you don't have your library card, I can use your photo ID."

She ignores me and continues to shuffle things around in the purse.

"I forgot my wallet," she says. "Can I still check out?"

"I'm sorry, only if you have your library card or an ID."
She sighs.
"Can't you look up my name?"
"No, I'm sorry, I can't check out to you without your library card or a photo ID."
And then she says it.
"The other *librarian let me…"*
I hope she doesn't notice my eye twitch.

Many librarians have worked with the *other* librarian—the cooler, more laid-back librarian. The librarian who thinks no harm could come if we didn't require a library card or photo ID to checkout. The librarian who wouldn't *care* if someone had an open drink near a computer. The librarian who would understand a phone on speaker isn't going to bother anyone.

But if we were to ask who the other librarian was or what they looked like?

"Oh…I don't know…" or "The one with the brown hair. You know, with glasses."

Those *other* librarians let patrons get away with a lot. They allow them to wander around the building without shoes or shirts. They don't care if patrons smoke in the bathrooms. They ignore eardrum-damaging headphone volumes. They extend computer sessions beyond the maximum time allowed.

Uh-huh. Sure.

Now don't get me wrong—I trust most patrons. But if they mention the *other* librarian, I'm bound to trust them as far as I can toss an unabridged copy of the *Oxford English Dictionary*.

On the other hand, there are those coworkers who do make everyone else's lives harder by not being consistent with policy. The *real* "other librarians." They let personal biases, favoritism, laziness, or lack of care for rules determine how and when they follow the book.

Don't have a library card or photo ID? No problem! Need extra time on the computer even though people are waiting? Sure! Want to check out more than the max number of DVDs? That's a silly rule anyway.

I am all for taking a situational approach to applying policy and making exceptions, especially when rules create unnecessary or unjust hurdles. However, there's a difference between conceding in certain situations and letting patrons walk all over you. It's still as frustrating for other staff to hear those three words, and if rules aren't applied consistently, we're going to hear them.

"The *other* librarian..." is only one of many phrases your average librarian would prefer not to hear you utter. I'd also recommend never asking anyone at a public service desk how long they've been "volunteering" at the library. Never mention anything about dog-earing pages, writing in books, or creasing spines. Be careful about comparing your current library to your last library.

Also, be warned: sentences that start with "As a taxpayer…" are likely to send a librarian into a fit of convulsions.

"So, how long have you been volunteering here?"

People often think of library work as something you only volunteer for in retirement. Quiet, slow-paced, stress-free—libraries are the perfect place to spend your golden years, right? (Again, if you're still under that misguided impression, please go back a few chapters.)

The truth is, though, that's not entirely false.

The operations of the libraries where I've worked are significantly supported by volunteers. When staff time is limited, volunteers help by shelving materials, assisting with children's programs, stamping withdrawn books, packaging interlibrary loan materials, and many other day-to-day tasks. They also run Friends of the Library and foundation organizations, which often host sales, events, or operate shops to support the library.

A good number of the people involved with the libraries in this capacity are retired librarians, teachers, or professors. But volunteering isn't just for retirees.

Depending on the availability of work, students can get experience and community service hours for graduation or scholarship requirements. Aging friends organizations are constantly seeking younger members to keep things running. And, if you have the time and are in a position financially to do so, volunteering is a great way to introduce yourself and demonstrate skills to hiring managers if you're looking to work at a library.

With all that said though, never assume someone shelving in the stacks, checking out items, or greeting patrons at a front desk is volunteering their time.

What's the big deal? Some may laugh or shrug it off, but when you assume a librarian is volunteering their time, you imply that their work isn't valuable. That they don't deserve to be paid for their time. It also undermines the fact that librarians provide necessary work for their communities, work for which not everyone is qualified.

We have skills that we've honed for this purpose. We invested in degrees, filled out applications, and interviewed to prove ourselves fit for a position, and we do deserve to be compensated. So, instead of asking, "How long have you been volunteering here?" perhaps ask, "How long have you been working here?"

"I'm a bad library patron"

It happens often.

You meet someone in a bar, coffee shop, the grocery store, and you casually let slip that you're a librarian. If they don't mention something about the Dewey Decimal System, cardigans, or TNT's *The Librarians* television series, they'll start to tell you all about how they're terrible library patrons.

"Oh, I haven't been to the library in years. Do they still exist?"

"I checked out *The Catcher in the Rye* in high school and never returned it."

"I owe so many fines!"

"My dog chewed up a book I checked out, and I just stuck it in the book drop. I've never been back."

It makes me wonder if people are like this with other professionals. Do they tell the doctors they meet at bars that they don't exercise or eat right? Do they admit to dentists at the grocery store that they don't brush or floss? Do they announce to mechanics that they regularly let their gas gauge fall below a quarter of a tank? I don't.

As much as it irks me to hear these admissions, I take it as an opportunity to proselytize for the library. Too many overdue fees? Most libraries will work with you on a payment plan, and many have even done away with the practice of charging them altogether. That book you never returned as a kid? Chances are, your account and the fine has been purged from the system for inactivity. Your pet chewed up a book? If you're willing to admit the damage and pay the replacement fee, we're happy.

Then there are the admissions from patrons at the library. Often, they're trying to be conversational and end up sharing too much information. They may not even realize what they're admitting is frowned upon.

"Oh, I'll have these books back way before the due date. I read constantly, even while I'm in the restroom."

"I'm pretty sure I've read that one. Check for my initials in the back. I mark every book I checkout."

"I don't need a bookmark. I'll just dog-ear the pages."

Somewhere a librarian's heart shrivels. Please, don't tell me you read library books in the restroom. You don't want to get me started on how unsanitary that is! And as innocuous as dog-earing pages and branding books may sound, I don't want to know you're damaging or defacing library books. I don't care what you do to the books you own, but these are the community's resources, not just yours!

"My last library..."

"My last library...." Now there's a tricky phrase. Depending on the context, it can either make a librarian's day or cause their eyes to roll.

I admit it. We love when you praise the library. We're all about hearing how the library we're working in is better than all the ones you've been to before.

"Wow, this place is so much bigger than my last library!"

"My last library didn't have nearly as many movies."

"The staff here is so much nicer!"

We pride ourselves in our buildings and the work we do, and it makes our day when patrons recognize it. However, it's a double-edged sword. When you praise a library by comparing it to your last, that means you're often tearing down that other library. Being on that negative side stinks, especially when we're told about it.

"I could check out twice as many movies at my last library."

"The chairs are much more comfortable at the other branch."

"The computers were way faster at my last library."

It's not that we don't appreciate the feedback. Libraries ideally are all about making sure that the needs of their communities are met and that patrons feel comfortable coming back. Nothing will ever change or improve if we're not told what's wrong or could be better. We listen.

I only suggest that comparing us to your last library isn't the best way to do that. Depending on the librarian's mood, you might just get told to go back there.

"I'm a tax-paying citizen..."

"...and I don't want my tax dollars being spent on..."

Yes, we get it. Public libraries are tax-funded organizations, and taxpayers should have some input on how funds are spent. But if a patron uses this line, they're either going to get the "smile and nod" response or an eye roll. When they're starting a complaint this way, there are a few things they're ignoring or not thinking about.

First, to be quite literal, an individual's annual tax contribution is a very small percentage of a public library's revenue. Even smaller is the percentage spent on materials or programming. Most tax dollars go to staff salaries, utility bills, and other operating expenditures. When someone is upset about their tax dollars being spent on one book, one display, one program, we're literally talking nickels and dimes.

Second, all tax-paying citizens support the library. That includes citizens of different ethnicities and economic backgrounds, LGBTQIA+ citizens, and citizens who hold different religious beliefs. Not just the wealthy, white, straight, Christian, cis-gendered citizens.

We hear the "my tax dollars" line often from those who don't believe the library should "promote alternative lifestyles" by having LGBTQIA+ books in the collection or offering inclusive programming like Drag Queen story hours. What about the tax dollars of LGBTQIA+ citizens? By the sheer majority, the library is filled with books and other materials that ignore, disparage, or condemn their existence. Why should that be the only viewpoint represented?

We also hear this line from those who think the library should have less "fluff" like popular movies and "low-brow" books, and that the library's computers should only be used for research. In their minds, library collections should have specific educational or literary value. They think kids shouldn't be allowed to play video games or be on Facebook on public computers when others might need to do schoolwork.

But public libraries shouldn't be in the business of determining what's of educational or literary value according to one segment of the population's opinion. Again, public libraries are for all citizens in their communities. It's written in the American Library Association's Bill of Rights: "Libraries should provide materials and information presenting all points of view on current and historical issues. Materials should not be proscribed or removed because of partisan or doctrinal disapproval."

Finally, not every dollar a public library spends is public. Private donations, grants, and funds raised by friends and foundation organizations support the library as well. That one book someone finds objectionable could have been donated. That program or event that one group thinks shouldn't take place at a public institution could be entirely funded by an outside organization. When people use the "my tax dollars shouldn't pay for this" line, it's always interesting to see their response when they're told, "Well, actually, they didn't."

Again, I may make it sound like libraries don't appreciate input from tax-paying citizens. That's not the case. But we can recognize when someone is honestly wanting to improve the library and when someone is using the "I pay my taxes" line to throw their weight around. What's especially fun is when someone says, "My tax dollars pay your salary."

You know what? Mine do too.

Asked on Facebook: What's your biggest librarian pet peeve?

So hopefully it's not a surprise to you that librarians have a few pet peeves. As much as we love our jobs and what we do, there are the little things that get to us, just like any other humans in any other job. While the best of us do well to not take the frustration out on patrons, call them out specifically, and get ourselves in trouble, sometimes it does help to vent in a space where we can relate to each other.

Here are other pet peeves shared on the *Librarian Problems* Facebook page:

Snapping fingers or yelling "hey" from across the room to get my attention. Please stand up and come to the desk to ask for help!

When patrons say their book donation is in good condition but actually it smells like dead people, is covered in spider webs, has coffee rings on the covers, is sticky (blech) or is full of handwritten notes and/or highlighting. Just...no.

People who initial or use some other cryptic code of dots to mark the books they've read.

Being expected to be what amounts to someone's unpaid office staff. I swear there's one customer who is a landlord that I think I'm owed about 25% of their income.

When they say to their child, "If you don't turn it in on time, she'll be mad at you!" I always make sure that the child understands that this is not the truth as I look the parent dead in the eye while explaining this horrible lie!

When patrons are ready to check out and they just throw down their library card without even saying a word. I'm like, "Uh, are you ready to check out?"

Having parents pick up their sick kids from school and the first thing they do is run here to check out movies for them as that sick child stands/lays on our counter spreading germs on everything.

People who call for a phone number and then when you start to tell them what it is, they say, "Oh wait, let me get a pen." Or who call to put a book on hold and don't have their library card at hand. It's not that hard, folks!

"Have you read 'XYZ book'? I can't believe you are a librarian and you have never read that book. You really need to read it." This frustrates me because

I have read so many books and I keep up with every-thing, but I can't read everything.

When patrons push all the books to the back of a shelf. "All of the books on all of the shelves have their spines lined up on the edge, but this one shelf we must have gotten wrong; here, let me fix them for you!"

Chapter 16
Joys of Librarianship

Okay, I'm done ranting.

After reading those last two chapters, you might be wondering if I hate my job. If I like to complain so much, wouldn't I be better off finding another?

That couldn't be further from the truth. I love what I do, I love working with the public, and I love what libraries are all about. Everyday I think I could pinch myself, because I feel like I'm dreaming. But, honestly, I wouldn't want to do that, because if it were a dream, I wouldn't want to wake from it.

However, I've long since accepted that no job is perfect. I'll always have responsibilities I don't enjoy, coworkers who I don't get along with, or days where

I want to call it early and go home. On her most stressful days, my administrative assistant at the Oskaloosa Library used to say she'd hitch a ride on the next semitruck that passed by and she'd be gone. Sometimes, I feel that so hard. But that doesn't mean I despise the job.

In case you need convincing, though, this chapter is dedicated to things that have brought me joy in this career. From fascinating research requests to positive patron interactions to finding my purpose, these are a few of the things that have made it all worthwhile.

The Joy of Research Requests

One of the first tasks at the Lawrence Public Library that I grew to love as a reference assistant was genealogy and local history research for patrons. Most of the time, I simply had to dig up obituaries for long-dead relatives. A little morbid, I know, but there was something about scanning through decades-old newspapers on the library's ancient microfilm readers that I just found fascinating. There was one request, though, that was unique.

I had just arrived for my morning shift and sat down to check my work email at a computer in the adult services office when Lynn handed me a thick envelope with the library's address scrawled across the lower left-hand corner in barely legible cursive.

"You like doing research, don't you?" I knew I was in for it by the tone of her voice.

"Uh, sure," I said. "What is this?"

"Take a look. I'm honestly surprised it made it to us," she said.

Postmarked from Santa Rosa, California, the lines of the return and receiving addresses slanted and curved into each other. Inside was a letter hand-written in the same shaky, curling script on both sides of several sheets of notebook paper.

"I got through most of the first page," Lynn said. "I think they're asking for information on the Eldridge Hotel."

"Is that it?"

"Well, there's twenty pages there. Good luck!"

As daunting as reading the letter may have seemed, I was instantly intrigued and up for the task. Known for alleged paranormal activity, the Eldridge had been featured on the show *My Ghost Story* on A&E's Biography Channel. The letter writer, a resident at a retirement home in Santa Rosa with Lawrence connections, must have watched the episode and had been moved to write a request for more information about the hotel as well as other historical details about Lawrence.

She specifically asked about Colonel Shalor Eldridge, who, according to the Spencer Research

Library at the University of Kansas, was a busi-
nessman that was active in making the territory of
Kansas a free state and who bought the land where
the current Eldridge Hotel sits at 701 Massachusetts
Street. I found these details in the article, "Ghosts
rumored to haunt site" published in the *Lawrence
Journal-World* on Wednesday, May 11, 2005.

The lot was home to the Free State Hotel, which
was destroyed by a pro-slavery mob, and the colonel
built what was known as the Eldridge House afterward. Some say it's his ghost that lingers there today.
The activity seems to center around the 5th floor,
where an original cornerstone resides, and some tell
tales of the old elevator (now no longer in the building) bringing them to this floor after they requested
others.

Most endearing was the writer's concern for the
colonel's spirit. She wrote:

> *I would like to know why Colonel Eldridge's ghost
> and spirit is still remaining and lingering and hang-
> ing around the hotel and haunting the hotel? Does he
> know…that he is dead and that his body was placed
> in a casket and buried in the grave?*

As I've no talent for communicating with spirits,
I couldn't find answers to those specific questions.

However, in the rest of the letter, she requested information on the history of Lawrence during the Civil War, the state of Kansas, any Native Americans that occupied the area, and any cemeteries, prisons, and forts in the area. When I explained this to Lynn, she recommended not spending too much time on the request.

"I imagine she'll be happy with a few articles," she said.

In my research, I found and printed a couple of stories and pictures from the *Lawrence Journal-World* as well as an excerpt from Beth Cooper's *Ghosts of Kansas* that summarized the paranormal history of the Eldridge Hotel. I also put together a list of books about Lawrence that she could read. I wrote a response explaining what I found and how she could request more information.

I didn't hear back from the letter writer, so I never learned whether she was satisfied with what we found for her. However, I appreciated that the request led me to investigate Colonel Eldridge's story. Having not grown up in Lawrence, I enjoyed the chance to learn a little more about the city's history in the process.

That's one reason why I love this job so much: I get so many opportunities to learn more.

The Joy of Weeding

Weeding is the process of culling the library's collection for outdated, poorly conditioned, or low circulating materials to discard. Those under the impression that librarians are incorrigible book lovers who cringe at the thought of throwing out books might be surprised that I would list this as a favorite part of the job. For me, though, earning this responsibility and the power that came with it was a sign that I had made it as a librarian.

As a part-time reference assistant at the Lawrence Library, weeding was not in my purview. That was reserved for the full-time librarians. Each had an assigned Dewey range or section of the fiction collection and would regularly receive a weeding list from the collection development coordinator.

Off-desk time being a scarce commodity, the librarians would load up a cart with selected volumes and review them during downtime at the reference desk. I would watch in wonder as they meticulously inspected the books and decided what to keep and what to discard. *Such responsibility!* I remember thinking.

That responsibility wouldn't be mine until nearly two years into my time at Lawrence. The city had passed an eighteen-million-dollar referendum to expand and renovate the library, and the collection team needed extra help weeding in preparation for the move to a temporary location. They didn't want to transfer or store anything unnecessary.

Finally, the power was mine!

Sometimes the general public doesn't understand the need or importance of weeding. People especially get up in arms when they see a library throwing out large quantities of books and materials at once. Even some librarians are less inclined to weeding collections, always foreseeing some value or need for titles to remain on the shelves.

But libraries, especially public libraries, simply don't have the space to keep every volume ever purchased. Over time, books become outdated, are superseded by new editions, fall into poor condition, or sit for years on the shelves without being touched. Why keep a worn copy of some one-time classic that no one has picked up in two years when you can make room for newer titles that do circulate? A regular, systematic weeding process keeps the shelves from becoming overcrowded, which in turn, keeps it easy to find and discover books.

When this process is neglected and new management arrives and sees a need for a major collection overhaul, that's when it becomes tricky. I ran into this at Oskaloosa. In her later years, the longtime children's librarian had shifted more and more of her focus to providing outreach services to pre-schools and elementary classrooms. On top of in-house programming and desk time, this left little room for collection maintenance for the one-person department.

When I started, the city manager made it clear something had to be done about the children's collection. Located on the basement level in a poorly lit area, the shelves were packed with titles dating back as far as the 1970s. It felt more like a sterile warehouse than an inviting children's library.

I wasn't about to immediately step in there, though, and start telling the children's librarian that she couldn't go read to children anymore so she could focus on the collection. Nor was I going to start throwing stuff out behind her back. I knew she felt pride in her job and the collection she had built over the years. I needed to plan carefully.

Incidentally, the situation solved itself, as she submitted her intent to retire not two months after I started. When interviewing applicants, I made sure to ask about collection maintenance experience and weeding philosophies.

Once on board, the new children's librarian developed a systematic cleanup plan. Eventually, she got the collection down to a point where we could remove some shelving to open the space, add some colorful carpeting, and arrange more face-out displays. Many of the books we withdrew went to a book sale, which in turn supported the acquisition of new titles, and the circulation of books that remained in the collection began to increase.

So, aside from the power I felt as a real librarian, that's what I appreciate about the process of weeding. Cleaning up the collection by removing items that are no longer needed or are no longer in good condition helps circulation increase, as it's easier to find and browse items on the shelf.

The Joy of Transforming Lives

When I was teaching computer classes at the Lawrence Library, there was one patron who consistently frowned throughout the sessions. She would rarely ask questions or make comments and always walked away like she was dissatisfied. I assumed she either didn't care for my teaching style or hated computers.

She kept signing up for classes though, and one day after a session, she said to me, "I almost deleted my Facebook account."

"Oh, why's that?" I asked.

"I didn't like having all my information out there," she said. "But then I got a friend request from someone I went on a mission trip with when

I was in college. I haven't heard from her in over twenty years."

"Wow! That's really great!"

"Yeah. You know, I hear a lot of bad things about Facebook and the Internet, but I think I see the good there too. Thank you for offering these classes."

That's what I loved the most about teaching computer sessions. The attendees were, for the most part, very grateful for the chance to learn something new. Even though I walked away from some classes scatter-brained and exhausted, working with patrons who were well into retirement and who still had a passion and curiosity for learning and improving their skills brought a lot of joy to my days.

The patron who I thought didn't care for the courses walked away with a better understanding of the site, which allowed her to connect and communicate with her friends and family more easily. Armed with the tools to protect her privacy, she was now more confident in those interactions and was able to enjoy the site as it was meant to be enjoyed. This is the kind of transformation that librarians and libraries make possible.

They happen every day. Whether it's a shy young patron who opens up when asked about their favorite book or someone researching overcoming addictions finding the resources that will help them or an avid mystery reader discovering a new favorite author because of conversation, librarians have the power to change peoples' lives. Transformations like these make being a librarian so rewarding.

The Joy of Providing Space to Be

In my first year at Oskaloosa, as the children's librarian and I prepared for the summer reading program, we asked the members of the teen advisory board what kinds of events they would like the library to offer for their age group. Among suggestions for movie nights, craft programs, chess clubs, and messy games, one teen suggested Dungeons & Dragons. I silently balked but wrote down the idea not wanting to discourage the teen. All ideas were welcome.

You see, my only experience with the tabletop role-playing game was in college. A friend who roomed two levels above mine in the dorms invited me to play with his group. They waited patiently as my friend and I spent nearly an hour setting up a character for me. I couldn't believe how much detail went into creating one, and how much game-related knowledge the guys had committed to memory.

Once the adventure commenced, I realized the time commitment involved and ducked out, coyly explaining that I had to use the restroom. I didn't have the nerve to tell them I wasn't interested in the game, so I went back to my room. After about an hour, my friend knocked on my door. "Hey, we've been wondering where you were. It's your turn."

Baffled, I admitted my crime.

I was willing to give the game a try at the library, though, so we scheduled two-hour Dungeons & Dragons sessions twice a month. My hesitation proved unwarranted.

The teen who suggested the program was one of six brothers, all of whom, save for the youngest toddler, played regularly at home. He agreed to lead the session as Dungeon Master, and I was surprised and delighted to see eight teens show up for the first adventure. It was the easiest, most low-key program, as all I had to do was provide the promised snacks and observe from the sidelines as the DM led the game.

Because attendance over the summer remained consistent and the teens who participated seemed to enjoy it, we agreed to continue the sessions into the fall and make it a weekly Saturday program. That's when it exploded.

The few teens who attended the summer sessions must have gone back to school and told all their friends about it. We started seeing twenty to twenty-five middle and high school students every week. A manageable company is about eight players, so we often had three adventures going simultaneously, led by the original DM and two of his brothers. I couldn't believe it! So many snacks were consumed.

Through observing the adventures unfold and admittedly participating as a half-giant named Vaunea, I learned that D&D is great for developing creativity, communication, and leadership skills. Otherwise reserved teens lit up and participated, or even led the adventures, with excitement. Everyone got along, and everyone was included.

The D&D session also sparked an increase in overall teen programming at the library. More teens started showing up at our craft programs, chess clubs, and the teen advisory board. We held annual messy games, zombie crawls, and ugly sweater parties, and summer reading participation increased.

Working with teens quickly became one of my favorite parts of my job, but one compliment made me realize how important teen programming can be.

At the last bash of one of the summer reading programs, one of our regulars thanked me for offering so many programs at the library. Having been one of the original D&D members, she was excited to start bringing her younger sister, who would be moving into the age group in the fall. She had been involved with the teen advisory board before I started at the library, and she appreciated how much more we were doing.

"The library's been like a second home this summer," she said. "I could come here when I didn't feel like I could be at home."

The Joy of Purpose

One morning when I was walking out the front doors of the Oskaloosa Library on my way to an annual budget meeting with the city manager and clerk, a patron stopped and greeted me. Out of nowhere, she said, "I'm so glad you're here and the library's here."

She couldn't have had a clue as to where I was headed, or how nervous I was about the meeting, but those words calmed my nerves. As she continued into the library, a weight lifted off my shoulders. Because of her words, any doubts about what I was asking the city for financially were quelled. I was armed with a greater sense of the library's value in the community.

Her comment also reminded me of my purpose. Whatever her reasons for her passion for the library, it was my job as director to ensure that she had access to the services and resources she needed. It was my job to justify expenditures and request funds from the city council so that the library could continue to provide those services and resources.

Books, CDs, DVDs, magazines—these things are sometimes viewed as frivolities to council members who have other ideas for taxpayer dollars. In my mind, though, it's easy to see how an investment in these items can save the community money. Storytimes, research help, computer classes, teen programs, author visits, presentations, and many other things beyond the physical items also add value to the library as a public service. But none of these would be possible without the library's most valuable asset: staff.

A significant portion of a library's budget goes toward staff salaries and benefits, and any cut to the budget could mean a cut to staff. As a director, I never wanted to see that. I was so grateful for the staff that I got to work with, and for all that they did to make the library what it was for the community. The library wouldn't be the same without their years of experience, their knowledge, and their positive customer service.

Having served as director helped me understand the value and purpose of every library position, from the pages to the facilities staff to the librarians. Now that I've moved on from that position and am no longer at the top of an organization, it still reminds me of why I do what I do: I love being a part of helping others learn and grow and be successful in whatever form that may be.

Chapter 17
This Isn't My Last Chapter

Ten years.

That's all the library experience I have behind me. Compared to those who've been in this field for decades, I'm just a newbie. I haven't seen nearly as many "librarian problems" as they have, and I acknowledge and own that.

I have nothing but respect for the librarians and library workers who've come before me—the movers and shakers, the staff who've dedicated half their lives or more to their organizations, and those who've helped transform libraries into what they are today.

This field has a fascinating history, and I'll never know what it was like to try to find a book title without the ease of a Google search, to check out items with due date slips and stamps, or to convert the physical card catalog to a computer database. I was still a kid when computers and the Internet began to transform the work of libraries.

So, as a way of "passing the mic" to those who have much more experience than I do, I'm closing this book with an interview with three colleagues who have been working at the Lawrence Public Library longer than I've been alive.

Sherri started in the reference department in 1984 and recently retired from her position as assistant director. Darla began working in circulation in 1983 and is currently an Assistant II in the accounts department, and Nancy has worked in cataloging since she earned a position out of high school in 1979.

Collectively, they have over 100 years of experience at the library. They've seen *all* the "librarian problems." However, when I sat down with them, I could tell they have as much passion and love for their jobs as I hope to have when I'm looking back on my career from where they are now.

They graciously answered a few questions for me and shared their library stories:

Tell me about your path to librarianship. What interested you in working at the library?

Sherri: Like many librarians, I graduated with a Bachelor of Arts in English and went out into the world looking for a job, and I thought, *What would this qualify me to do?* After I worked a few office jobs, one with Camp Fire Girls [of America], I thought about what I might want to do, and librarianship seemed like a good fit. I liked the idea of being associated with learning, but there was a part of me that wanted to help, to be in service work, and that seemed like a nice blend of things. I also thought I would do lots of research. Maybe, in the beginning, I did some, but I never really did a whole lot of what you would really think of as research. But you learn. You learn and you adapt.

Darla: I loved to read since an early age. I remember going to the library down at the Carnegie building when I was a little kid and going to the children's department down in the basement. Then when I was in grade school, in fifth and sixth grades, I worked in the library as a student aide. I did not do it in junior high. That librarian wasn't overly friendly and didn't encourage you to come to the library. Then in high school, my mom was real good friends with the librarian there and was close with a lady who worked for her. My junior and senior year I was a student aide in the library, and then when I graduated from high school, the assistant to the librarian had surgery and was out for six weeks, so I took her place for six weeks. From there I was hired at LPL. I think I was just meant to be in the library.

Nancy: My older sister worked for the Lawrence Public Library for a short period of time while she was in high school. I was about seven or eight at the time and would often play "library" with my own personal books, creating my own pockets and checkout cards, while dreaming of how fun it would be to work at a library.

When I was a senior in high school, I was enrolled in a class called *Office Education*. This class was for a two-hour period every day where we worked on practicing basic office skills. Sometime during the first semester, our teacher would find local part-time jobs that would match the individual student's strongest office skills. At this time, the school held an ongoing job placement spot with the Lawrence Public Library, in what was then called Cataloging and Processing. The *Office Education* employee would work a minimum of two hours per day at this designated job during the entire school year.

My dream came true when I was asked to apply and interview with the Lawrence Public Library as a job clerk in the Cataloging and Processing department. My job duties included: typing check-out cards and pockets, typing the subject headings on the tops of card catalog card sets, filing, and placing Mylar over the original book covers before they were sent into circulation. I was in love! I had a fantastic job with more choices of books to read than I had time! After my year was over, I was offered a full-time job in the Cataloging Department, and the library gracefully bowed out of the *Office Education* job placement program. My one-year part-time job turned into a lifetime career.

What was your career path? What positions have you held, and where are you now?

Sherri: I got my degree at Emporia State because it was the handiest and most affordable place to get your library degree back then. I stayed on for a year at the college library while my husband finished up his degree, and I worked in the reserves department for a year. Then we moved, and I found the job at the reference department at the Lawrence Public Library, and little did I know that 35 years later, I'd still be there.

When the interlibrary loan position opened, I took that on, partly because it was one of the few jobs where you got to use a computer at the time. Catalogers had them, and then they were starting to sneak in a few other places. I thought, "I really want to learn this. This is exciting!" And I have to say I didn't mind a more regular schedule. Once I did that, I didn't have to work nights and weekends, except occasionally. That was kind of nice as a mom.

We finally got an online catalog in 1996, I think. The catalog itself was the core of what we were doing technology-wise then, and I became the assistant system administrator for the catalog for a while. I did that at the same time I did interlibrary loan, and mostly it just meant I knew how to do some basic things if the coordinator was gone. And it was another way to learn a little bit about how computers operate.

Then the assistant director position came open in, I think around 2000, and I applied for that. I just kind of stayed put in that role, which ended up being changeable in and of itself depending on what the crisis of the moment was, filling in as department heads in different departments occasionally. Then when we built the new library, I managed the move. It just morphed into whatever needed to be done when there wasn't a logical place for anyone to do it.

Darla: I started out as a page. At that time when you checked out, it was all on microfilm. You would take the patron's library card and the card out of the back of the book, and we had a stack of due-date cards that were in numerical order. You'd take a picture to put on microfilm. Then you'd take the top card off, with the due date, and put in the back of the book with the title card.

My position then that I got, I would put all those cards in order when they came back, cut new ones if there were ones missing, and stamp the new due date on them. You stamped probably 4,000 to 6,000 a week. When you put them in order, you would write down the numbers of the ones that were missing, and you would look up on the microfilm by that number and type up a little overdue slip.

From there, I went to the full-time desk position in Adult Circulation. I worked the front desk 40 hours a week. I checked things out to people, and I checked things in. I sent out notices for their holds that were ready for them to pick up. I took money for payments, and I sent out the overdue fine notices. From that, I went to the clerical job in Adult Circulation. I would collect the due date cards and would write down the ones that came in overdue on the date. You had to wait until the film filled up and you'd send it off to get it developed, so you would run at least a month behind on due dates and notices. If it hadn't been back yet, I'd go out to the shelf to see if we hadn't missed it.

I held that position, I don't know for how long. I'm on my third director. I had three department heads. Then I became Materials Handling Coordinator, and now I'm back in Accounts.

Nancy: Forty years later, I'm still in Cataloging and Processing, but it is now referred to as the Cataloging Department. I am a cataloging assistant, cataloging collections for music CDs (juvenile and adult), movie DVDs and Blu-rays, board books, and large print fiction.

Libraries have evolved significantly since you began your career. What are the changes that stand out most to you?

Sherri: Technology has obviously driven a lot of it. When I started, we were still on the old paper card catalog, and I do remember we were a little slow to get an automated system. When we finally did, the wonder of key word searching! I started in 1984, and one of the popular titles of that year was *The Hunt for Red October* by Tom Clancy. All these people wanted to read it, but no one could remember the title. It was his first book, and nobody knew his name yet. They might have the first letter right, and they might have Clancy, but they might not. They knew "red" was in it. We had it, but you couldn't find it because, back then, if they didn't have a few words right at the beginning of the title, we couldn't find it in the catalog until we became more familiar with the title. Key word searching was a huge thing!

Darla: Going computerized really made things a lot easier and made things a lot quicker. When we weren't computerized, you couldn't call to renew things over the phone. There was just no way of doing it. We also would have to type up holds on cards, and every time we had a cart, we had to go pull a drawer and double check it against everything on the cards, and if you had a book that had a hold, you'd pull the card and put it in the book and set it to the side. So that made it slower to get your holds. With the computerized system, when you check it in, it tells you there's a hold.

Nancy: When I started my job, the library was using a card catalog for our patrons. Every morning before the library opened, I filed cards into the card catalog. Today, I sit at my desk, using a computer, and import electronic cataloging records into our catalog. Patrons can find everything they need with a few simple keystrokes on a computer, laptop, or even a smart phone.

What are some of your favorite library memories?

Sherri: Being involved in hiring and then seeing the people that you hire grow and take on more responsibilities and become these fabulous librarians with so much to give our library or maybe some other library. To see them grow in their careers and know I had a little part in getting them started. That's a happy thought and a satisfying one.

My all-time favorite memory is just because of the total absurdity of it. Fairly early on when I started working in reference, we had a local guy around town. Everyone knew Bob, and Bob liked to play what I would call "stump the librarian." He would catch you at the reference desk, or wherever, and would ask you a question that he knew the answer to, but that you probably didn't. He was one of those few patrons where you would see someone else engaged with him for a while, and if it went on for too long, you might go to the back and call them, and give them an opportunity to break the conversation.

The thing I remember about Bob is that it was a Saturday, as I recall, and I was working the reference desk. He comes in and he plops on the desk this dead animal. It was small and kind of furry, and he threw it on the desk and said, "What's that?" And of course, he knew what it was. I had no clue. I think it might have been a woodchuck. He had found it along the side of the road, probably a victim of roadkill, but it was in pretty good shape. It was whole. It wasn't bloody or anything like that. It wasn't gross. It was a cute little dead animal that he threw on my desk. That's my most memorable moment with Bob.

Darla: One of the things that really amused me was when we would go out and find liquor bottles shelved in among the books. You wouldn't realize it was a bottle of liquor until you went to touch it. That was always fun to go out and find those.

I was shifting books one time, and when I moved a big section of them, I found a huge pile of cigarette butts. I don't know how we never smelled them, and how patrons never started a fire dumping them behind the books.

We would play tricks on our supervisor when she was gone. Working the circulation desk isn't always a fun job because people yell at you, so we would try to devise ways to make the job fun. One time when she was gone, we filled her office with balloons. Underneath her desk, in the cabinets so every time she opened the cabinets, balloons would fall out. She had to move balloons to get into her desk. They were everywhere. Our favorite trick was when we made it the gates of hell because she came back on Halloween. We took red tissue paper and taped it around the light fixtures, so it looked like flames and gave off a red glow. Then we took black paper and made a gate. She actually had to take a patron back there to discuss a problem, and needless to say he didn't argue with her much!

Nancy: When I first started my job in 1979, the library had circulating collections of LP records, audiocassettes, and framed art prints. The art prints were checked out for one month and seemed to be a big hit with our patrons. At the time, some staff were trying to convince the library director to remove these collections from the library, arguing that patrons want to come to the library to check out books, not record albums, art prints, and audiocassettes! Soon thereafter, we weeded the art prints, followed by the audiocassettes, and then our LP record collection went last.

I sit back and smile to myself, as some staff today get really excited (as they should) when there is discussion about offering our patrons collections like board games, S.A.D. lamps...items other than "just books!"

Any personal "Librarian Problems" stories?

Sherri: There was someone who insisted they had to have a photograph of Jesus. Not an artistic rendering, but a photograph. That was what they wanted us to find for them.

I remember once, this was pre-Internet, Dean Koontz had a book, and at the heading of each chapter he had a poem, and people kept wanting to know if it was a real thing or if it was something he made up. We used all our poetry books and all our resources, but we couldn't find anything definitive one way or the other. So I wrote him a letter, and he—or someone on his team —responded and told us it was indeed something he had made up and it did not exist. People wanted us to confirm, because if it existed, they wanted to read the whole thing, but it was something he had created for this book. That was fun.

There was a potato gun that people wanted instructions for how to make. It was hard to get a hold of. I think we had to interlibrary loan a book and photocopy the pages for them. Then we kept them because potato guns were apparently a thing then.

There was the censorship issue with Madonna's book. She put out a book that created all kinds of stir in the library world. People didn't think we should have it. We had it.

Darla: I had a taxidermy book come back soaked with chemicals. Obviously, they were reading it as they were doing their taxidermy.

Before we remodeled, and when I first started, in the entryway from the parking lot was the smoking area. So you could go sit there and read your book and smoke. Then the building went nonsmoking, so you could still go over there and sit and read your book, but you couldn't smoke. We had a group of people who made it their living room and brought in a portable TV and plugged it in the outlet that was right across from the couch and chairs. They'd sit there and watch TV and yell at people who walked by because it blocked their view! We'd have to go tell them they couldn't do that.

Nancy: Many, many years ago, during the era of VHS movie cassettes, I received a VHS in a plastic ziplock bag with a note from our circulation department saying a patron returned this item with cockroaches in it. The note indicated they wanted me, the person in charge of AV mending, to double-check to see that it was ok to return to our collection. Boy was I surprised, when, keep in mind, this was many days later, I opened up the ziplock bag, pulled out the VHS, removed the screws with my special screw driver, popped it apart, and watched a couple of cockroaches run out! I believe that is the most memorable "surprise" story I've encountered during my library career.

Do you have any advice for aspiring librarians, or those getting started?

Sherri: There are a lot of jobs in libraries where you don't need a library degree, and it's a good way to get an experience to see what working in a library is like. A library degree is an investment, and sometimes it's not always what you think. In a public library, you should like working with people of all kinds and all sorts because that's who we work with, and it can be the most satisfying thing if that's what you like. If it's just working with books that's most interesting to you, there are certain types of library jobs that are like that, but a lot of what we do is very people-oriented, and I don't think that's necessarily what a lot of people think of with libraries.

Darla: You have to have a good sense of humor. Be able to go with the flow. Be kind to everyone, and don't take yourself too seriously.

Nancy: Libraries, a place where you start with an *interest* in a *job* but end up with a *career* you are *passionate* about. Best unexpected adventure of my life!

And finally, because we're librarians, I must ask, what are some of your favorite books?

Sherri: One of my favorite authors, at least in recent years, has been Wallace Stegner. *Crossing to Safety, Angle of Repose*—I really like his work. I also like to escape and get into whole other worlds, and I read a lot of mysteries. I'm not too much into the cats and cakes and clever puns, but I especially like the British procedurals. I always like to go back and read some Jane Austen and reread those classics that when you read them at different times of your life, they're like completely different books.

We have a readers' advisory team, and they talk a lot about what it is that appeals to you about books, and for me, a lot of times it's the characters. You can learn a lot about people through fiction, and I think that's one of the things I enjoy about reading.

Darla: I wrote some down! Nina Wright, the *Whiskey Mattiome Mystery Series*, I love those. Then Mary Higgins Clark, Shirley Jackson,

Tim Dorsey, Lisa Lutz—her *Spellman* series, and of course Agatha Christie. True crime like *In Cold Blood* and *Helter Skelter*, and I just now started getting into Manga.

Nancy: I don't so much have a favorite book, but I do have several favorite authors: Ann Rule, Jill Shalvis, and Debbie Macomber.

Chapter 18

Final Words and New, Bigger Problems

I originally envisioned ending this book with the words and stories of Sherri, Darla, and Nancy. What better way, I thought, to acknowledge that I'm not the only one with "librarian problems," and that my own "problems" maybe aren't all that bad?

Then I learned about what those in the publishing and printing industry call a signature—a group of pages that, when printed upon and folded or bound together, make up a section of a book. My editor noted that, due to how signatures work at certain printers, my book would incur about a dozen blank pages in the back. I couldn't have that, so you get more problems!

Now that I think of it, I didn't tell the story about the patron who, in the middle of a computer class, decided to remove their shoes and socks and apply ointment to their feet. Oh, or the time I came across another clipping their toenails with their bare foot propped on a table! And did I happen to mention how often patrons try to hand us library cards they just had in their mouths, or worse, undergarments?

Actually, that reminds me. I should really take this opportunity to address a much bigger problem that libraries (not to mention humanity as a whole) have recently faced: a worldwide pandemic. The SARS-CoV-2 coronavirus and COVID-19 literally put a stop to business as usual, and, in most cases, library operations were no exception.

I turned in the initial draft of this book on March 1, 2020, two weeks before the Lawrence Public Library halted storytimes, programs and events and eventually shut its doors to the public as directed by the county health department. Along with schools, community buildings, recreation centers, and other public facilities, the library was rightfully deemed a risk for spreading the coronavirus.

Up to that point, as cases began to arise and then exponentially increase in cities across the United

States, the library's leadership team had pretty much worked on its toes planning how to meet this new challenge. You see, we couldn't find the section in our disaster preparedness manual on worldwide pandemics. It actually hadn't even been written!

In socially distanced meetings in the library's auditorium (picture a huge circle of 6-foot tables, one staff member per table), we discussed how we would keep patrons and staff safe if we were allowed to stay open, what services and programs would look like if we were required to close, whether staff would be required to take earned leave time, and what necessary operations would need to continue to ensure communication wasn't disrupted, digital resources were still available, and the building was secure.

Staff who weren't high-risk continued to work in the building the week after we closed, shelving returns, processing new materials, placing orders, and finishing low-priority projects. By the end of March, though, the governor of Kansas issued a statewide stay-at-home order, and staff were told to stay home unless absolutely necessary.

We stopped taking returns from patrons, paused ordering to reduce deliveries, and moved what we could online. Our Youth Services team began planning and offering live storytimes on Facebook, Readers' Services transitioned their book club meetings to Zoom, Collection Development focused on ramping up digital collections, and the leadership team continued to meet weekly virtually to check in on operations and prepare for eventual reopening.

The case for closing libraries

We were privileged at LPL. As an independent taxing district and not a department of the city, the library's personnel and financial decisions remain with the library director and board of trustees, and they elected to continue paying staff regularly expected wages. Those who were able to work remotely were encouraged to do so, while staff whose responsibilities relied on being in the building were asked to focus on taking care of their families and selves.

From following several librarians and library workers on Twitter, I knew that others weren't so fortunate. If they weren't required to work in libraries that remained open to the public, they were furloughed or even laid off. Those forced to work (or otherwise take leave time) justly decried having to do so in unsafe conditions, especially in communities and metropolitan areas that were seeing the highest number of cases and mortality rates. The hashtags #ClosetheLibraries and #ProtectLibraryWorkers began trending with stories from frustrated, scared, and exhausted library workers at these organizations.

Being handed a card that was in someone's mouth is just one example of a disease vector in a busy library. At LPL, we get hundreds of visitors a day—visitors of all ages who sit in crowded computer labs, browse the shelves, handle materials, play video games with shared controllers, talk with each other, and sit for hours on end. For busier libraries in much larger cities, the vectors must be uncountable.

On the Kansas library listserv, a few directors of much smaller libraries argued, though, that it shouldn't be a "one size fits all" solution. Small rural libraries staffed by one or two at most don't see the kind of traffic that bigger city libraries do. It's much easier to clean and sanitize surfaces, trace interactions, and remain socially distant in small libraries.

On the other hand, the coronavirus doesn't distinguish between library sizes. All it would take is one asymptomatic carrier to contract the virus on a monthly trip to a big box store in the city and visit and infect and incapacitate the library staff. Where would they be then?

The impact of closing isn't lost on me. Wandering through a darkened LPL, it was difficult to see a place once lively with the hum of activity, a place that brings joy, enlightenment, and reprieve to so many in the community, suddenly inaccessible. People who depend on us for the Internet, restrooms, and shelter have limited to no alternatives. But we were doing our part in preventing the spread of COVID-19 in our community and keeping our local health-care system from getting dangerously overwhelmed.

Even though libraries have spent the last thirty years, at least, trying to convince stakeholders, politicians, and government leaders that our institutions are essential to our communities, especially in times of crisis, the crisis of a pandemic is different. Closing the library meant saving lives.

Reopening in the "new normal," whatever that looks like

As we moved into May and June, and community leaders, health officials, and state governors felt pressure to end stay-at-home orders to "save the economy," leadership at LPL began carefully planning phases for reopening. Even though the city's and county's infection rates remained much lower than those of surrounding communities of similar or larger sizes, we opted to start slow.

The issue remained a hot topic on #LibraryTwitter. What frustrated librarians and library workers the most were experts who claimed that going to the library was a relatively low-risk activity. In one online article, "From hair solons to gyms, experts rank 36 activities by coronavirus risk level" published on mlive.com on June 8, 2020, experts assigned libraries a risk level of 3 out of 10. To quote the article, "These aren't typically super crowded areas and often have larger spaces and higher ceilings, which helps lower the risks."

Are you kidding me? That description might have fit more libraries fifty years ago, but not today!

Even Phase 1 of the Governor of Kansas's plan indicated that libraries were okay to open, with the caveat that local health departments could maintain stricter regulations. Despite that, leadership at LPL decided to start with offering curbside pick-up by appointment only in Phase 1, and after two weeks, opened the building for limited access to pick up holds for a second phase.

At the time of my writing this chapter, we're only now looking at what Phase 3 will look like and have many questions and concerns. Are we ready to open the building for browsing? Can we effectively limit the number of patrons in the building and how long they stay? How can we enforce social distancing, or is it even possible? Where do we stand, as public institutions, in requiring that patrons wear masks? How long will these guidelines be necessary?

We're all in the same ~~boat~~ storm

A part of me regrets ending what was meant to be

a light-hearted analysis of libraries and librarianship on such a somber note. I'm just one librarian
with a limited perspective from one small part of
the world, but I hope my words here can offer some
semblance of hope.

I've appreciated a new take on an old idiom that's
been quoted by so many politicians, writers, leaders,
and social media accounts recently that it's hard to
trace its origins: "We're not in the same boat, we're
in the same storm."

When it comes to resources, staff, and the communities they serve, every public library is unique.
Some are consistently well funded while others
struggle each year with shoestring budgets and the
threat of cuts. Some are housed in modern, expansive, eco-friendly buildings, while others remain in
outdated public facilities with ailing infrastructure.
Some have little to no staffing issues, while others
experience burnout, low morale, poor management,
and more.

Whatever the differences, *all* libraries are facing
the COVID-19 pandemic. One of our life preservers
at LPL has been reaching out to other institutions
and library professionals to learn how they have
been responding to the pandemic to help inform our
own plans. Knowing we can draw on the wisdom,

knowledge, and experience of others has strengthened our resolve.

That, to me, is essentially what libraries have been about from the beginning: access to information to improve lives. As long as we learn from and support each other, we'll get through this pandemic together to the new normal—whatever that may look like.

Acknowledgments

Now, seriously, *these* are my final words.

To be honest, I agreed to write 40,000 words, and since my first round of edits cut out about 500, I needed to make up that difference. Who knew turning GIFs into a book would be such a challenge? My solution: Acknowledgments!

Anyway, I'd like to thank, first, those who made it possible for me to live my dream as ~~Forney Hull~~ a librarian:

Lynn, you gave me my first library job. Thank you for believing in my abilities as an inexperienced library school student and rescuing me from having to make pizza in a gas station for the rest of my life. For that I will forever be grateful.

To the members of the Oskaloosa Public Library Board of Trustees (in 2012) and the Oskaloosa City Manager, thank you for putting your trust and your library in the hands of a 27-year-old. I had a lot of fun. Oh, and learned a lot.

Polli, thank you for helping me get my foot back in the door at LPL. My stint as a readers' services assistant and member of the Book Squad was brief but meaningful.

And Tricia, thank you for challenging me with the role of LPL's Cataloging and Collection Development Coordinator even though my experience as a cataloger was not quite up to par. I love leading my team, and that, I'm sure you would agree, is what matters most.

Speaking of teams, my gratitude also goes out to both my previous staff at the Oskaloosa Public Library and my current team of catalogers, collection development librarians, and one acquisitions assistant. I'm so grateful for what you do, for your passion for your work, and for your dealing with my scatterbrained self as your supervisor.

Who else?

My *Librarian Problems* fanbrarians! Thank you for following my Tumblr, Twitter, and/or Facebook page, and sharing your stories with me. Your likes, reblogs, and comments helped get *Librarian Problems* where it is today. I would be remiss not to acknowledge that. I hope to continue sharing content with you, and maybe meet you someday. So, say "Hey" if you bump into me at a conference or library event!

I'd also like to thank Julie at Skyhorse Publishing and Jamie at the American Library Association for helping me make this book as best as it can be.

Lastly, I'd like to thank Nate. The last ten years with you have been great, and I thank you for pushing me to finish this little project.

About the Author

William Ottens is a librarian from Lawrence, Kansas and creator of the library-centric Librarian Problems Tumblr. Described by Library Journal's Tumblr-in-Chief, Molly McArdle, as the GIF-king of all librarian tumblrs, William's Librarian Problems blog pairs common librarian situations, frustrations, and stereotypes with animated reaction GIFs. His public library experience includes work in reference, administration, cataloging, and collection development. He served as Director of the Oskaloosa Public Library in Oskaloosa, Iowa from 2012 to 2015, and is currently the Cataloging and Collection Development Coordinator at the Lawrence Public Library in Lawrence, Kansas.